AF575671

Publications International, Ltd.

Louis Weber, CEO
Publications International, Ltd.
8140 Lehigh Ave
Morton Grove, IL 60053

Pictured on the front cover: Chocolate Chip Pizza Cookie *(page 182)*

Pictured on the back cover *(clockwise from top left):* Frittata Rustica *(page 12),* Renegade Steak *(page 94)* and Lemon Garlic Roast Chicken *(page 55).*

ISBN: 978-1-63938-152-4

Manufactured in China.

8 7 6 5 4 3 2 1

Microwave Cooking: Microwave ovens vary in wattage. Use the cooking times as guidelines and check for doneness before adding more time.

WARNING: Food preparation, baking and cooking involve inherent dangers: misuse of electric products, sharp electric tools, boiling water, hot stoves, allergic reactions, foodborne illnesses and the like, pose numerous potential risks. Publications International, Ltd. (PIL) assumes no responsibility or liability for any damages you may experience as a result of following recipes, instructions, tips or advice in this publication.

While we hope this publication helps you find new ways to eat delicious foods, you may not always achieve the results desired due to variations in ingredients, cooking temperatures, typos, errors, omissions or individual cooking abilities.

TABLE OF CONTENTS

Spanikopita Pull-Aparts

(page 154)

CAST IRON CRASH COURSE

Cast iron pans have been around for hundreds of years, so why all the fuss about them now? The answer is simple: As more people are cooking at home, they're rediscovering this old-fashioned cookware and its many strengths. Cast iron is incredibly versatile, durable and inexpensive—what's not to like?

WHY CAST IRON?

There are many great reasons to own a cast iron skillet (or several!):

LONGEVITY

Simply put, this pan will last a lifetime. It's easy to find home cooks using their grandmothers' and great-grandmothers' pans; these are often handed down from generation to generation. A quick search on eBay will show you how the value of these older pans has gone up over time.

DURABILITY

It is virtually impossible to put a dent in a cast iron pan. There are no rivets or welded joints to wear out because the pan is cast from a mold in a single piece of metal. And with a good layer of seasoning, it's also impervious to rust and scratches. You can heat it over the highest flames on your stovetop, stick it under the broiler or put it right into the coals of a campfire; the pan will be none the worse for the wear.

VERSATILITY

The range of dishes you can make in this pan is incredible. Start with breads such as corn bread, cinnamon rolls, biscuits or even pizza. Cook up bacon, eggs and hash for hearty breakfasts. Sear meat and seafood beautifully, or fry chicken to perfection. And don't forget dessert! Skillet pies, crisps and cookies are a delicious way to end any meal.

HEAT RETENTION

Dense cast iron pans do take a long time to heat up—far longer than other metals used in cookware such as aluminum or copper. But they don't cool down much when food is added, and they maintain a steady heat so foods cook and brown evenly. The heat in the pan also stays constant in the oven, where temperatures often fluctuate during baking.

NATURAL NONSTICK COATING

A brand new, pre-seasoned pan might not be perfectly nonstick right out of the box, but after regular use, a layer of seasoning will build up and the surface will be as nonstick and smooth as a Teflon-coated pan—without all the chemicals.

INEXPENSIVE

Unless you want to pay a high price for a vintage pan, you can find a large cast iron skillet for around $30 or even less. Compared to the expensive, high-end cookware on the market today, cast iron is an exceptional bargain!

THE PAN THAT CAN...

Fry: Everyone loves fried chicken, but the bird is just the beginning. There are so many other tempting options to explore, from fritters, dumplings and doughnuts to hush puppies and potatoes. Cast iron makes frying simple and foolproof.

Sear: Your cast iron pan is the secret to getting a beautifully browned crust on steak, chicken, pork, burgers, scallops and more. Whether you're cooking a big roast for a crowd or individual fillets, the results are consistently delicious.

Sauté: Almost everything you need for a weeknight meal can be sautéed in a cast iron pan—chicken for quesadillas, vegetables for a stir-fry, blackened shrimp for a po' boy sandwich, sausages for a quick skillet meal, etc.

Braise: For tougher cuts of meat, low and slow is the way to go. Hearty braised dishes such as short ribs, pork shoulder and beef stew are ideal cast iron comfort foods.

Bake/Roast: The ability of cast iron to go from stovetop to oven means the recipe possibilities are endless. You can sear a steak or fish fillet on the stove, then finish cooking it in the oven. You can cook sweet or savory fillings on the stove, top them with a pie crust and bake them in the oven. Or go straight to the oven for beautiful roasted vegetables, whole chicken, fluffy biscuits or an old-fashioned fruit crisp.

Broil: If you want to cook a steak or fish fillet in a flash, brown the top of a frittata or get a good crust on a burger without a grill, your cast iron pan and your broiler make a dynamic duo in the kitchen. Chicken and shellfish also fare well under the broiler, and even vegetables—especially peppers, tomatoes and chilies—can get a great smoky charred flavor in minutes.

CAST IRON MAINTENANCE

The best way to keep your cast iron pan in good condition is to use it often. You may have heard that cast iron is difficult to care for, but the basics are actually very simple.

- Clean the skillet immediately after using it—it is much easier to remove stuck-on food from a hot pan than a cold one. (Just don't soak the pan or leave it in the sink.)
- Wash the pan by hand using hot water and a soft sponge. Opinions vary widely about using soap—many believe that soap will strip a pan's seasoning, but others argue that a small amount of today's mild dish soap is completely harmless. Both sides agree that tough abrasives, such as steel wool, rough scouring pads or kitchen cleansers, should always be avoided.
- For any stubborn food residue, scrub the pan with a paste of coarse salt and water or coarse salt and oil. You can also loosen stuck-on food by boiling water in the pan for several minutes.
- When the pan is clean, dry it thoroughly, reheat it and coat the inside of the pan with a thin layer of oil using a paper towel or a cloth. Store the pan in a dry place.

SEASONING CAST IRON

How does seasoning work? The surface of a cast iron pan is full of tiny cracks, pores and irregularities that food sticks to when cooking. The key to preventing this sticking is fat: When oil is heated in the pan, it polymerizes, which means it forms a dense, slick layer on the surface that makes it seem nonstick. The more times oil is reheated in a pan, the thicker this layer gets.

The vast majority of new cast iron cookware sold today is pre-seasoned, so this additional seasoning process may not be necessary. However, new pre-seasoned cast iron pans will have some sticky spots at first; you can help build up the seasoning by cooking fatty foods the first few times you use the pan.

1. Start out with a clean, completely dry pan. (At this point you can wash the pan with soap since it will be seasoned afterwards.)
2. Rub all surfaces of the pan (inside and outside) with a thin layer of vegetable oil, canola oil, corn oil or shortening using a paper towel or a cloth.
3. Heat the pan in a 450°F oven for 30 minutes or until the surface has darkened in color.
4. Repeat the oiling and heating process three more times until the pan is very dark black. Let the pan cool before storing it in a dry place.

BREAKFAST & BRUNCH

STRAWBERRY-TOPPED PANCAKES

- 1½ cups sliced fresh strawberries
- 2 tablespoons seedless strawberry jam
- 1¼ cups all-purpose flour
- ¼ cup sugar
- 1 teaspoon baking powder
- 1 teaspoon baking soda
- ¼ teaspoon salt
- 1¼ cups buttermilk
- 1 egg, lightly beaten
- 1 to 2 tablespoons vegetable oil
- Whipped cream (optional)

1. Combine strawberries and strawberry jam in medium bowl; stir gently to coat. Set aside while preparing pancakes.
2. Combine flour, sugar, baking powder, baking soda and salt in large bowl; mix well. Add buttermilk and egg; whisk until blended.
3. Heat 1 tablespoon oil in large cast iron skillet over over medium heat. For each pancake, pour ½ cup batter into skillet, spreading into 5- to 6-inch circle. Cook 3 to 4 minutes or until bottom is golden brown and small bubbles appear on surface. Turn pancake; cook 2 minutes or until golden brown. Add additional oil to skillet as needed.
4. For each serving, stack three pancakes; top with strawberry mixture. Serve with whipped cream, if desired.

Makes 2 servings (6 large pancakes)

CHORIZO-POTATO HASH

1 naan or pita bread, torn into pieces

6 tablespoons plus 1 teaspoon olive oil, divided

Coarse salt and black pepper

1 pound Mexican chorizo sausage, casings removed

1 onion, diced

1 yellow bell pepper, diced

1 red bell pepper, diced

2 russet potatoes, peeled, grated, rinsed and squeezed dry *or* 1 package (20 ounces) refrigerated shredded hash brown potatoes

1 green onion, diagonally sliced

1. Place naan in food processor; pulse about 15 times or until small crumbs form. Transfer to medium bowl. Add 2 tablespoons oil; toss to coat.
2. Heat large cast iron skillet over medium heat. Add crumb mixture; cook 6 to 8 minutes or until browned and toasted, stirring occasionally. Season with salt and black pepper; return to bowl.
3. Heat 1 teaspoon oil in same skillet over medium-high heat. Add chorizo; cook 5 minutes or until browned, using spatula to break up meat. Transfer to paper towel-lined plate.
4. Heat 1 tablespoon oil in same skillet. Add onion and bell peppers; cook 8 minutes or until vegetables are tender, stirring occasionally. Season with salt and black pepper. Transfer to large bowl.
5. Heat remaining 3 tablespoons oil in same skillet. Add potatoes in even layer; cook 3 minutes or until browned and beginning to crisp on bottom. Turn potatoes, cook 10 minutes or until tender and evenly browned, stirring occasionally. Season with salt and black pepper. Stir in chorizo and vegetable mixture; cook 2 minutes or until heated through. Top with bread crumbs and green onion.

Makes 6 servings

FRITTATA RUSTICA

- 4 ounces cremini mushrooms, stems trimmed, cut into thirds
- 1 tablespoon olive oil, divided
- ½ teaspoon plus ⅛ teaspoon salt, divided
- ½ cup chopped onion
- 1 cup packed chopped stemmed lacinato kale
- ½ cup halved grape tomatoes
- 4 eggs
- ½ teaspoon Italian seasoning
- Black pepper
- ⅓ cup shredded mozzarella cheese
- 1 tablespoon shredded Parmesan cheese
- Chopped fresh parsley (optional)

1. Preheat oven to 400°F. Spread mushrooms on small baking sheet; drizzle with 1 teaspoon oil and sprinkle with ⅛ teaspoon salt. Roast 15 to 20 minutes or until well browned and tender.
2. Heat remaining 2 teaspoons oil in small (6- to 8-inch) cast iron skillet over medium heat. Add onion; cook and stir 5 minutes or until soft. Add kale and ¼ teaspoon salt; cook and stir 10 minutes or until kale is tender. Add tomatoes; cook and stir 3 minutes or until tomatoes are soft. Stir in mushrooms.
3. Preheat broiler. Whisk eggs, remaining ¼ teaspoon salt, Italian seasoning and pepper in small bowl until well blended.
4. Pour egg mixture over vegetables in skillet; stir gently to mix. Cook 3 minutes or until eggs are set around edge, lifting edge to allow uncooked portion to flow underneath. Sprinkle with mozzarella and Parmesan.
5. Broil 3 minutes or until eggs are set and cheese is browned. Cut into wedges. Garnish with parsley.

Makes 2 servings

BAKED APPLE PANCAKE

- 3 tablespoons butter
- 3 medium Granny Smith apples (about 1¼ pounds), peeled and cut into ¼-inch slices
- ½ cup packed dark brown sugar
- 1½ teaspoons ground cinnamon
- ½ teaspoon plus pinch of salt, divided
- 4 eggs
- ⅓ cup whipping cream
- ⅓ cup milk
- 2 tablespoons granulated sugar
- ½ teaspoon vanilla
- ⅔ cup all-purpose flour

1. Melt butter in medium (8-inch) cast iron skillet over medium heat. Add apples, brown sugar, cinnamon and pinch of salt; cook 8 minutes or until apples begin to soften, stirring occasionally. Spread apples in even layer in skillet; set aside to cool 30 minutes.
2. After apples have cooled 30 minutes, preheat oven to 425°F. Whisk eggs in large bowl until foamy. Add cream, milk, granulated sugar, vanilla and remaining ½ teaspoon salt; whisk until blended. Sift flour into egg mixture; whisk until batter is well blended and smooth. Set aside 15 minutes.
3. Stir batter; pour evenly over apple mixture. Place skillet on rimmed baking sheet in case of drips (or place baking sheet or piece of foil in oven beneath skillet).
4. Bake 16 minutes or until top is golden brown and pancake is loose around edge. Cool 1 minute; loosen edge of pancake with spatula, if necessary. Place large serving plate or cutting board on top of skillet and invert pancake onto plate. Serve warm.

Makes 2 to 4 servings

CINNAMON PECAN ROLLS

- **4 tablespoons (½ stick) butter, melted, divided**
- **1 loaf (16 ounces) frozen bread dough, thawed according to package directions**
- **½ cup packed dark brown sugar**
- **2 teaspoons ground cinnamon**
- **½ cup chopped pecans**

1. Brush large (10-inch) cast iron skillet with ½ tablespoon melted butter. Roll out dough into 18×8-inch rectangle on lightly floured surface.
2. Combine brown sugar, 3 tablespoons butter and cinnamon in medium bowl; mix well. Brush mixture evenly over dough; sprinkle with pecans. Starting with long side, roll up dough jelly-roll style; pinch seam to seal.
3. Cut crosswise into 1-inch slices; arrange slices cut sides up in prepared skillet. Cover loosely; let rise in warm place 30 minutes or until doubled in size.
4. Preheat oven to 350°F. Brush tops of rolls with remaining ½ tablespoon butter.
5. Bake 20 to 25 minutes or until golden brown. Serve warm.

Makes about 18 rolls

BRATWURST SKILLET BREAKFAST

- **1½ pounds red potatoes**
- **3 bratwurst links (about 12 ounces), cut into ¼-inch slices**
- **2 tablespoons butter**
- **1½ teaspoons caraway seeds**
- **4 cups shredded red cabbage**

1. Cut potatoes into ¼- to ½-inch pieces. Place in large microwavable dish; cover and microwave on HIGH 3 minutes. Stir potatoes; microwave 2 minutes or just until tender.
2. Cook sausage in large cast iron skillet over medium-high heat 8 minutes or until browned and cooked through. Remove to paper towel-lined plate. Drain off drippings.
3. Melt butter in same skillet. Add potatoes and caraway seeds; cook 6 to 8 minutes or until potatoes are golden brown, stirring occasionally.
4. Return bratwurst to skillet; stir in cabbage. Cover and cook 3 minutes or until cabbage is slightly wilted. Uncover; cook and stir 3 to 4 minutes or just until cabbage is tender.

Makes 4 servings

STUFFED HASH BROWNS

- 1½ cups shredded potatoes*
- 2 tablespoons finely chopped onion
- ¼ plus ⅛ teaspoon salt, divided
- ⅛ teaspoon black pepper
- 2 tablespoons butter, divided
- 1 tablespoon vegetable oil
- ½ cup diced ham (¼-inch pieces)
- 3 eggs
- 2 tablespoons milk
- 2 slices (about 1 ounce each) American cheese

**Use refrigerated shredded hash brown potatoes or grated peeled russet potatoes, squeezed dry.*

1. Preheat oven to 250°F. Place wire rack over baking sheet. Combine potatoes, onion, ¼ teaspoon salt and pepper in medium bowl; mix well.
2. Heat 1 tablespoon butter and oil in small (6- to 8-inch) cast iron skillet over medium heat. Add potato mixture; spread to cover bottom of skillet evenly, pressing down gently with spatula to flatten. Cook 10 minutes or until bottom and edges are golden brown. Cover skillet with large inverted plate; carefully flip hash browns onto plate. Slide hash browns back into skillet, cooked side up. Cook 10 minutes or until golden brown. Slide hash browns onto prepared wire rack; place in oven to keep warm while preparing ham and eggs.
3. Melt 1 teaspoon butter in same skillet over medium-high heat. Add ham; cook and stir 2 to 3 minutes or until lightly browned. Remove to plate.
4. Whisk eggs, milk and remaining ⅛ teaspoon salt in small bowl. Melt remaining 2 teaspoons butter in same skillet over medium-high heat. Add egg mixture; cook 3 minutes or just until eggs are cooked through, stirring to form large, fluffy curds. Place cheese slices on top of eggs; remove from heat and cover skillet with lid or foil to melt cheese.
5. Place hash brown on serving plate; sprinkle one side of hash brown with ham. Top ham with eggs; fold hash brown in half.

Makes 1 to 2 servings

TIP **Refrigerated shredded potatoes are very wet when removed from the package. For the best results, dry them well with paper towels before cooking.**

DUTCH BABY PANCAKE

- 3 tablespoons butter, divided, plus additional for serving
- ½ cup all-purpose flour
- 2 tablespoons granulated sugar
- ¼ teaspoon salt
- ½ cup whole milk, at room temperature
- 2 eggs, at room temperature
- ¼ teaspoon vanilla
- Powdered sugar
- Lemon wedges

1. Preheat oven to 400°F. Place 1 tablespoon butter in large (9- to 10-inch) cast iron skillet; place skillet in oven to heat while preparing batter. Melt remaining 2 tablespoons butter in small bowl; let cool slightly.
2. Combine flour, granulated sugar and salt in medium bowl; mix well. Add milk, eggs, melted butter and vanilla; whisk 1 minute or until batter is very smooth.
3. Remove skillet from oven; immediately pour batter into hot skillet.
4. Bake about 20 minutes or until outside of pancake is puffed and edges are deep golden brown. Sprinkle with powdered sugar; serve with lemon wedges and additional butter.

Makes 2 servings

BREAKFAST BISCUIT BAKE

- 8 ounces bacon, chopped
- 1 small onion, finely chopped
- 1 clove garlic, minced
- ¼ teaspoon red pepper flakes
- 5 eggs
- ¼ cup milk
- ½ cup (2 ounces) shredded white Cheddar cheese, divided
- ¼ teaspoon salt
- ⅛ teaspoon black pepper
- 1 package (16 ounces) refrigerated jumbo buttermilk biscuits (8 biscuits)

1. Preheat oven to 425°F. Cook bacon in large cast iron skillet until crisp. Remove to paper towel-lined plate. Drain off and reserve drippings, leaving 1 tablespoon in skillet.
2. Add onion, garlic and red pepper flakes to skillet; cook and stir 5 minutes or until onion is softened. Set aside to cool slightly.
3. Whisk eggs, milk, ¼ cup cheese, salt and black pepper in medium bowl until well blended. Stir in onion mixture.
4. Wipe out any onion mixture remaining in skillet; grease with additional drippings, if necessary. Separate biscuits and arrange in single layer in bottom of skillet. (Bottom of skillet should be completely covered.) Pour egg mixture over biscuits; sprinkle with remaining ¼ cup cheese and cooked bacon.
5. Bake 25 minutes or until puffed and golden brown. Serve warm.

Makes 8 servings

SPINACH FETA FRITTATA

- 6 eggs
- ⅓ cup evaporated milk
- 1 package (10 ounces) frozen chopped spinach, thawed and squeezed dry
- ½ cup finely chopped green onions
- 1½ teaspoons dried oregano or basil
- ½ teaspoon salt
- ⅛ teaspoon black pepper
- 2 cups cooked spaghetti (4 ounces uncooked)
- 4 ounces crumbled sun-dried tomato and basil or plain feta cheese
- 1 tablespoon olive oil
- Diced red bell pepper (optional)

1. Preheat broiler.
2. Whisk eggs and evaporated milk in medium bowl until well blended. Stir in spinach, green onions, oregano, salt and black pepper. Stir in spaghetti and cheese; mix well.
3. Heat oil in medium (8-inch) cast iron skillet over medium heat. Add egg mixture; cook 5 minutes or until almost set, stirring occasionally.
4. Broil 3 to 5 minutes or until frittata is just beginning to brown and center is set. Garnish with bell pepper. Cut into wedges.

Makes 4 servings

SWEET POTATO PANCAKES

PANCAKES

- 2 medium sweet potatoes
- 2½ cups all-purpose flour
- 1 teaspoon baking powder
- 1 teaspoon baking soda
- ½ teaspoon salt
- ½ teaspoon ground cinnamon
- ¼ teaspoon ground ginger
- 2¾ cups buttermilk
- 2 eggs
- 2 tablespoons packed brown sugar
- 2 tablespoons butter, melted and cooled, plus additional for pan

GINGER BUTTER

- ¼ cup (½ stick) butter, softened
- 1 tablespoon packed brown sugar
- 1 teaspoon grated fresh ginger
- Pinch salt
- Prepared caramel sauce or maple syrup
- ¾ cup chopped glazed pecans*

**Glazed or candied pecans may be found in the produce section of the supermarket along with other salad convenience items, or they may be found in the snack aisle.*

1. Preheat oven to 375°F. Scrub sweet potatoes; bake 50 to 60 minutes or until soft. Cool slightly; peel and mash. Measure out 1⅓ cups for pancake batter.
2. Combine flour, baking powder, baking soda, salt, cinnamon and ground ginger in medium bowl; mix well. Whisk buttermilk, eggs and 2 tablespoons brown sugar in large bowl until well blended. Stir in 2 tablespoons melted butter. Add sweet potatoes; whisk until well blended. Add flour mixture; stir just until dry ingredients are moistened and no streaks of flour remain. Do not overmix; batter will be lumpy. Let stand 10 minutes.
3. Heat large cast iron skillet over medium heat; brush with melted butter to coat. For each pancake, pour ½ cup batter into skillet, spreading into 5- to 6-inch circle. Cook 4 minutes or until bottom is golden brown and small bubbles appear on surface. Turn pancake; cook 3 minutes or until golden brown. Add additional butter to skillet as needed.*
4. For ginger butter, beat ¼ cup softened butter, 1 tablespoon brown sugar, fresh ginger and pinch of salt in small bowl until well blended. If using caramel sauce, microwave according to package directions. Stir in water, 1 teaspoon at a time, to thin to desired pouring consistency.
5. Serve pancakes warm topped with ginger butter, caramel sauce and glazed pecans.

**Since pancakes are large, a skillet may not be able to cook more than one at a time. Keep pancakes warm in 250°F oven on wire rack set over baking sheet.*

Makes 5 servings (10 large pancakes)

BREAKFAST MIGAS

- 1 small ripe avocado, diced
- 1 tablespoon lime juice
- 1 tablespoon olive oil
- 1 small onion, chopped
- 1 jalapeño pepper, seeded and diced
- 3 corn tortillas, cut into 1-inch pieces
- 1 medium tomato, halved, seeded and diced
- 6 eggs
- 2 tablespoons chunky salsa
- Salt and black pepper
- 1 cup (4 ounces) shredded Monterey Jack cheese

1. Combine avocado and lime juice in small bowl; toss to coat.
2. Heat oil in large cast iron skillet over medium heat. Add onion and jalapeño; cook and stir 1 minute or until softened. Add tortillas and tomato; cook about 2 minutes or until tomatoes are soft and heated through.
3. Whisk eggs and salsa in small bowl; season with salt and black pepper. Pour mixture into skillet; cook until eggs are firmly scrambled, stirring occasionally.
4. Remove skillet from heat; stir in cheese. Top each serving with avocado.

Makes 6 servings

NOTE Migas, a Mexican breakfast dish, is traditionally made in a skillet with leftover, stale tortillas that are torn into small pieces.

APPETIZERS & SNACKS

MOZZARELLA IN CARROZZA

- 2 eggs
- ⅓ cup milk
- ¼ teaspoon salt
- ⅛ teaspoon black pepper
- 8 slices country Italian bread
- 8 to 12 fresh basil leaves, torn
- 8 oil-packed sun-dried tomatoes, drained and cut into strips
- 6 ounces fresh mozzarella, cut into ¼-inch slices
- 1½ tablespoons olive oil

1. Whisk eggs, milk, salt and pepper in shallow bowl or baking dish until well blended.
2. Place four bread slices on work surface. Top with basil, sun-dried tomatoes, cheese and remaining bread slices.
3. Heat oil in large cast iron skillet over medium heat. Dip sandwiches in egg mixture, turning and pressing to coat completely. Add sandwiches to skillet; cook 5 minutes per side or until golden brown. Cut into strips or squares.

Makes about 8 appetizer servings

TIP **To serve these sandwiches as a snack or lunch instead of an appetizer, cut them in half instead of strips or squares.**

TEX-MEX NACHOS

- 1 tablespoon vegetable oil
- 8 ounces ground beef
- ½ cup chopped onion
- 2 cloves garlic, minced
- 2 teaspoons chili powder
- 1 teaspoon ground cumin
- ½ teaspoon salt
- ½ teaspoon dried oregano
- 1 can (about 15 ounces) kidney beans, rinsed and drained
- ½ cup corn
- ½ cup sour cream, divided
- 2 tablespoons mayonnaise
- 1 tablespoon lime juice
- ¼ to ½ teaspoon chipotle chili powder
- ½ bag tortilla chips
- ½ (15-ounce) jar Cheddar cheese dip, warmed
- ½ cup pico de gallo
- ¼ cup guacamole
- 1 cup shredded iceberg lettuce
- 2 jalapeño peppers, thinly sliced into rings

1. Heat oil in large cast iron skillet over medium-high heat. Add beef, onion and garlic; cook and stir 6 to 8 minutes or until beef is no longer pink. Add chili powder, cumin, salt and oregano; cook and stir 1 minute.
2. Stir in beans and corn. Reduce heat to medium-low; cook 5 minutes or until heated through.
3. Combine ¼ cup sour cream, mayonnaise, lime juice and chipotle chili powder in small bowl; mix well. Pour chipotle sauce into small plastic squeeze bottle.
4. Spread tortilla chips on platter or large plate. Top with beef mixture; drizzle with cheese dip. Top with pico de gallo, guacamole, remaining ¼ cup sour cream, lettuce and jalapeños. Squeeze chipotle sauce over nachos. Serve immediately.

Makes 4 to 6 servings

SMOKY BACON MUSHROOM TOASTS

- 8 slices bacon
- 1 onion, diced
- 1 red bell pepper, diced
- 2 packages (8 ounces each) mushrooms, diced
- Salt and black pepper
- 24 (½-inch) toasted French bread slices
- Chopped fresh parsley

1. Cook bacon in large cast iron skillet over medium heat until crisp. Remove to paper towel-lined plate. Drain off all but 2 tablespoons drippings from skillet.
2. Add onion and bell pepper to skillet; cook and stir over medium-high heat 3 minutes or until vegetables begin to soften.
3. Add mushrooms; season with salt and black pepper. Cook and stir 8 to 10 minutes or until mushroom liquid is almost evaporated. Cool 5 minutes.
4. Crumble bacon. Spread 1½ tablespoons mushroom mixture on each bread slice; sprinkle with crumbled bacon and parsley.

Makes 24 appetizers

CHICKEN LETTUCE WRAPS

- **1 tablespoon vegetable oil**
- **1 small onion, finely chopped**
- **5 ounces cremini mushrooms, finely chopped (about 2 cups)**
- **1 pound ground chicken**
- **¼ cup hoisin sauce**
- **2 tablespoons soy sauce**
- **1 tablespoon rice vinegar**
- **1 tablespoon sriracha sauce**
- **1 tablespoon oyster sauce**
- **2 cloves garlic, minced**
- **1 teaspoon grated fresh ginger**
- **1 teaspoon dark sesame oil**
- **½ cup finely chopped water chestnuts**
- **2 green onions, thinly sliced**
- **1 head butter lettuce**

1. Heat vegetable oil in large cast iron skillet over medium-high heat. Add onion; cook and stir 2 minutes. Add mushrooms; cook 8 minutes or until lightly browned and liquid has evaporated, stirring occasionally.
2. Add chicken; cook 8 minutes or until no longer pink, stirring to break up meat. Stir in hoisin sauce, soy sauce, vinegar, sriracha, oyster sauce, garlic, ginger and sesame oil; cook 4 minutes. Add water chestnuts; cook and stir 2 minutes or until heated through. Remove from heat; stir in green onions.
3. Separate lettuce leaves. Spoon about ¼ cup chicken mixture into each lettuce leaf. Serve immediately.

Makes 6 to 8 servings

TOASTED RAVIOLI

- 1 cup all-purpose flour
- 2 eggs
- ¼ cup water
- 1 cup plain dry bread crumbs
- 1 teaspoon Italian seasoning
- ¾ teaspoon garlic powder
- ¼ teaspoon salt
- ½ cup grated Parmesan cheese
- 2 tablespoons finely chopped fresh parsley
- Vegetable oil for frying
- 1 package (12 to 16 ounces) meat or cheese ravioli, thawed if frozen
- Pasta sauce, heated

1. Place flour in shallow bowl. Whisk eggs and water in another shallow bowl. Combine bread crumbs, Italian seasoning, garlic powder and salt in third shallow bowl. Combine cheese and parsley in large bowl; stir to blend.
2. Heat 2 inches of oil in large cast iron skillet over medium-high heat to 350°F; adjust heat to maintain temperature.
3. Coat ravioli with flour. Dip in egg mixture, letting excess drip back into bowl. Roll in bread crumb mixture to coat.
4. Working in batches, carefully add ravioli to hot oil; cook 1 minute or until golden brown, turning once. Remove from oil with slotted spoon; drain on paper towel-lined plate. Add to bowl with cheese mixture; toss to coat. Serve with warm pasta sauce.

Makes 20 to 24 ravioli

CAULIFLOWER SOCCA

- 2 cups chickpea flour
- 1¾ teaspoons salt
- ¼ teaspoon black pepper
- 2 cups water
- ½ cup olive oil, divided
- 1½ cups finely chopped cauliflower
- 1 can (about 15 ounces) chickpeas, rinsed and drained
- 2 tablespoons chopped fresh cilantro or parsley

1. Whisk chickpea flour, salt and pepper in large bowl to remove any lumps. Whisk in water and ¼ cup oil until well blended and smooth. Let batter stand at room temperature 30 minutes.
2. Meanwhile, preheat oven to 450°F. Place large (12-inch) cast iron skillet in oven to preheat at least 10 minutes.
3. Pour remaining ¼ cup oil into hot skillet. Add cauliflower and chickpeas. Bake 10 minutes.
4. Whisk cilantro into batter; pour batter over cauliflower and chickpeas in skillet. Bake 15 minutes or until edge is lightly browned, top is firm and toothpick inserted into center comes out with moist crumbs. Cut into wedges; serve warm or at room temperature.

Makes 8 servings

CHICKEN PARMESAN SLIDERS

- 4 boneless skinless chicken breasts (6 to 8 ounces each)
- ¼ cup all-purpose flour
- 2 eggs
- 1 tablespoon water
- 1 cup Italian-seasoned dry bread crumbs
- ½ cup grated Parmesan cheese
- Salt and black pepper
- Olive oil
- 12 slider buns (about 3 inches), split
- ¾ cup marinara sauce
- 6 tablespoons Alfredo sauce
- 6 slices mozzarella cheese, cut into halves
- 2 tablespoons butter, melted
- ¼ teaspoon garlic powder
- 6 tablespoons pesto

1. Preheat oven to 375°F. Line baking sheet with foil; top with wire rack.
2. Pound chicken to ½-inch thickness between two sheets of waxed paper or plastic wrap with meat mallet or rolling pin. Cut each chicken breast crosswise into three pieces about the size of slider buns.
3. Place flour in shallow bowl. Beat eggs and water in second shallow bowl. Combine bread crumbs and Parmesan in third shallow bowl. Season flour and egg mixtures with pinch of salt and pepper. Coat chicken pieces lightly with flour, shaking off excess. Dip in egg mixture, letting excess drip back into bowl. Roll in bread crumb mixture to coat. Place on large plate; let stand 10 minutes.
4. Heat ¼ inch oil in large cast iron skillet over medium-high heat. Add chicken in single layer (cook in two batches if necessary); cook 3 to 4 minutes per side or until golden brown. Remove chicken to wire rack; bake 5 minutes or until cooked through (165°F). Remove rack with chicken from baking sheet.
5. Arrange slider buns on foil-lined baking sheet with bottoms cut sides up and tops cut sides down. Spread 1 tablespoon marinara sauce over each bottom bun; top with piece of chicken. Spread ½ tablespoon Alfredo sauce over chicken; top with half slice of mozzarella. Combine butter and garlic powder in small bowl; brush mixture over top buns.
6. Bake 3 to 4 minutes or until mozzarella is melted and top buns are lightly toasted. Spread ½ tablespoon pesto over mozzarella; cover with top buns.

Makes 12 sliders

CHORIZO QUESADILLAS

- 1 package (9 ounces) Mexican chorizo sausage, casings removed
- 1 cup coarsely chopped cauliflower
- 1 small onion, finely chopped
- 12 (6-inch) flour tortillas
- 1½ cups (6 ounces) chihuahua cheese
- 6 teaspoons vegetable oil
- Salsa, guacamole and sour cream (optional)

1. Heat medium cast iron skillet over medium-high heat. Add chorizo, cauliflower and onion; cook and stir 10 to 12 minutes or until cauliflower is tender. Remove to bowl. Wipe out skillet.
2. Spread ¼ cup chorizo mixture onto each of six tortillas. Top with ¼ cup cheese and remaining tortillas.
3. Heat 1 teaspoon oil in same skillet over medium-high heat. Add one quesadilla; cook 2 to 3 minutes per side or until well browned and cheese is melted. Repeat with remaining oil and quesadillas. Cut into wedges; serve with salsa, guacamole and sour cream, if desired.

Makes 6 servings

TIP **To keep cooked quesadillas warm, arrange on a baking sheet and place in a preheated 200°F oven until all the quesadillas are cooked and ready to serve.**

CRAB CAKES CANTON

- 7 ounces fresh, frozen or pasteurized crabmeat or imitation crabmeat
- 1½ cups fresh whole wheat bread crumbs (about 3 slices)
- ¼ cup thinly sliced green onions
- 1 clove garlic, minced
- 1 teaspoon minced fresh ginger
- 2 egg whites, lightly beaten
- 1 tablespoon teriyaki sauce
- 2 tablespoons vegetable oil
- Prepared sweet and sour sauce
- Pickled ginger and green onion slivers (optional)

1. Pick out and discard any shell or cartilage from crabmeat. Combine crabmeat, bread crumbs, sliced green onions, garlic and ginger in medium bowl; mix well. Add egg whites and teriyaki sauce; mix well.
2. Shape mixture into patties about ½ inch thick and 2 inches in diameter.*
3. Heat 1 tablespoon oil in large cast iron skillet over medium heat. Add half of crab cakes; cook 2 minutes per side or until golden brown. Remove to serving plate; keep warm. Repeat with remaining 1 tablespoon oil and crab cakes.
4. Serve crab cakes with sweet and sour sauce; garnish with pickled ginger and green onion slivers.

**Crab cakes may be made ahead to this point; cover and refrigerate up to 24 hours before cooking.*

Makes 12 cakes

WHITE SPINACH QUESO

- 1 tablespoon olive oil
- 1 clove garlic, minced
- 1 tablespoon all-purpose flour
- 1 can (12 ounces) evaporated milk
- ½ teaspoon salt
- 2 cups (8 ounces) shredded Monterey Jack cheese, divided
- 1 package (10 ounces) frozen chopped spinach, thawed and squeezed dry
- Optional toppings: pico de gallo, guacamole, chopped fresh cilantro and queso fresco
- Tortilla chips

1. Preheat broiler.
2. Heat oil in medium saucepan over medium-low heat. Add garlic; cook and stir 1 minute without browning. Add flour; whisk until smooth. Add evaporated milk in thin, steady stream, whisking constantly. Stir in salt. Cook about 4 minutes or until slightly thickened, whisking frequently.
3. Add 1½ cups Monterey Jack cheese; whisk until smooth. Stir in spinach. Pour into medium cast iron skillet; sprinkle with remaining ½ cup Monterey Jack cheese.
4. Broil 1 minute or until cheese is melted and browned in spots. Top with pico de gallo, guacamole, cilantro and queso fresco. Serve immediately with tortilla chips.

Makes 4 to 6 servings

LEMON GARLIC SHRIMP

- ¼ cup olive oil
- 2 tablespoons butter
- 1 pound large raw shrimp, peeled and deveined (with tails on)
- 3 cloves garlic, crushed
- 2 tablespoons lemon juice
- ½ teaspoon paprika
- ¼ teaspoon salt
- Black pepper
- 2 tablespoons finely chopped fresh Italian parsley
- Crusty bread, sliced

1. Heat oil and butter in large cast iron skillet over medium-high heat until butter melts and mixture sizzles. Add shrimp and garlic; cook and stir 4 to 5 minutes or until shrimp are pink and opaque.
2. Add lemon juice, paprika, salt and pepper; cook and stir 1 minute. Remove from heat; discard garlic.
3. Spoon shrimp and skillet juices into large serving bowl; sprinkle with parsley. Serve with crusty bread for dipping.

Makes 6 to 8 servings

POULTRY

LEMON GARLIC ROAST CHICKEN

- 4 fresh rosemary sprigs, divided
- 6 cloves garlic, divided
- 1 lemon
- 2 tablespoons butter, softened
- 2 teaspoons salt, divided
- 2 large russet potatoes, cut into ¾-inch pieces
- 2 onions, cut into 1-inch pieces
- 2 tablespoons olive oil
- ½ teaspoon black pepper
- 1 whole chicken (3 to 4 pounds)

1. Preheat oven to 400°F. Finely chop 2 rosemary sprigs (about 2 tablespoons). Mince 3 cloves garlic. Grate peel from lemon. Combine butter, chopped rosemary, minced garlic, lemon peel and ½ teaspoon salt in small bowl; mix well. Set aside while preparing vegetables.
2. Combine potatoes, onions, oil, 1 teaspoon salt and ½ teaspoon pepper in medium bowl; toss to coat. Spread mixture in single layer in large cast iron skillet.
3. Smash remaining 3 cloves garlic. Cut lemon into quarters. Season cavity of chicken with remaining ½ teaspoon salt. Place garlic, lemon quarters and remaining 2 rosemary sprigs in cavity; tie legs with kitchen string, if desired. Place chicken on top of vegetables in skillet; spread butter mixture over chicken.
4. Roast 1 hour or until chicken is cooked through (165°F) and potatoes are tender. Let stand 10 minutes before carving. Sprinkle with additional salt and pepper to taste.

Makes 4 servings

JAMBALAYA PASTA

- 1 pound boneless skinless chicken breasts, cut into 1-inch pieces
- 2 tablespoons plus 1 teaspoon Cajun seasoning, divided
- 1 tablespoon vegetable oil
- 8 ounces bell peppers (red, yellow, green or a combination), cut into ¼-inch strips
- ½ medium red onion, cut into ¼-inch strips
- 6 ounces medium raw shrimp, peeled and deveined
- 2 cloves garlic, minced
- 1 teaspoon salt
- ¼ teaspoon black pepper
- 1½ pounds plum tomatoes (about 6), cut into ½-inch pieces
- 1 cup chicken broth
- 1 package (16 ounces) fresh or dried linguine, cooked and drained
- Chopped fresh parsley

1. Combine chicken and 2 tablespoons Cajun seasoning in medium bowl; toss to coat.
2. Heat oil in large cast iron skillet over medium-high heat. Add chicken; cook and stir 3 minutes.
3. Add bell peppers and onion; cook and stir 3 minutes. Add shrimp, garlic, remaining 1 teaspoon Cajun seasoning, salt and black pepper; cook and stir 1 minute.
4. Stir in tomatoes and broth; bring to a boil. Reduce heat to medium-low; cook 3 minutes or until shrimp are pink and opaque. Serve over hot pasta; sprinkle with parsley.

Makes 4 servings

TURKEY MOZZARELLA SANDWICH

BACON JAM

- 1 pound thick-cut bacon, chopped
- 2 large onions, chopped (about 1 pound)
- ⅓ cup packed brown sugar
- ⅛ teaspoon red pepper flakes
- ⅔ cup water
- ¼ cup coffee
- 1½ tablespoons balsamic vinegar

GARLIC AIOLI

- ¼ cup mayonnaise
- 1 clove garlic, minced
- 1 teaspoon lemon juice
- ⅛ teaspoon salt

PANINI

- 2 (6- to 7-inch) round focaccia breads, split
- 2 plum tomatoes, cut into ¼-inch slices
- 6 ounces sliced fresh mozzarella (¼-inch-thick slices)
- 6 ounces thickly sliced turkey breast (about ¼-inch-thick slices)
- ½ cup baby arugula

1. For bacon jam, cook bacon in large cast iron skillet over medium-high heat 10 to 15 minutes or until bacon is cooked through but still chewy (not crisp), stirring occasionally. Remove bacon to paper towel-lined plate. Drain off all but 1 tablespoon drippings from skillet.
2. Add onions to skillet; cook 10 minutes, stirring occasionally. Add brown sugar and red pepper flakes; cook over medium-low heat 18 to 20 minutes or until onions are deep golden brown. Stir in bacon, water and coffee; cook over medium heat 25 minutes or until mixture is thick and jammy, stirring occasionally. Stir in vinegar.*
3. For garlic aioli, combine mayonnaise, garlic, lemon juice and salt in small bowl; mix well.
4. Spread bottom halves of focaccia with garlic aioli. Top with tomatoes, cheese, turkey and arugula. Spread top halves of focaccia with bacon jam; place over arugula. Serve immediately.

**Recipe makes about 1½ cups bacon jam. Store remaining jam in refrigerator up to 2 weeks; return to room temperature before serving.*

Makes 2 to 4 servings

CHICKEN MADEIRA

- 4 boneless skinless chicken breasts (about 6 ounces each)
- ½ teaspoon salt
- ¼ teaspoon black pepper
- 3 tablespoons butter, divided
- 1 tablespoon olive oil
- 8 ounces mushrooms, sliced
- 1½ cups Madeira wine
- 1½ cups beef broth
- 8 ounces fresh asparagus, trimmed
- ¼ cup plus 1 tablespoon water, divided
- 1 tablespoon cornstarch
- 4 slices (about 1 ounce each) mozzarella cheese

1. Pound chicken to ¼-inch thickness between two pieces of waxed paper or plastic wrap with meat mallet or rolling pin. Season with salt and pepper.
2. Heat 1 tablespoon butter and oil in large cast iron skillet over medium heat. Add chicken; cook 4 to 5 minutes per side or until lightly browned. Remove to plate; tent with foil. Add 1 tablespoon butter and mushrooms to skillet; cook 8 minutes or until mushrooms are browned and liquid has evaporated, stirring occasionally and scraping up browned bits from bottom of skillet. Remove mushrooms to medium bowl.
3. Add Madeira and broth to skillet; bring to a boil over high heat. Reduce heat to medium; cook 10 to 12 minutes or until reduced by half.
4. Meanwhile, preheat broiler. Place asparagus in medium microwavable dish with ¼ cup water; cover with vented plastic wrap. Microwave on HIGH 4 minutes or until crisp-tender.
5. Stir remaining 1 tablespoon water into cornstarch in small bowl until smooth. Whisk into reduced liquid in skillet; cook and stir 2 minutes or until thickened. Add remaining 1 tablespoon butter; stir until melted. Stir in cooked mushrooms.
6. Place chicken on medium baking sheet; top with cheese and asparagus. Broil 2 minutes or until cheese is melted. Remove chicken to serving plates; top with sauce.

Makes 4 servings

BBQ CHICKEN SKILLET PIZZA

- **1 loaf (16 ounces) frozen bread dough, thawed**
- **1 tablespoon olive oil**
- **2 cups shredded cooked chicken***
- **¾ cup barbecue sauce, divided**
- **¼ cup (1 ounce) shredded mozzarella cheese**
- **¼ cup thinly sliced red onion**
- **½ cup (2 ounces) shredded smoked Gouda cheese**
- **Chopped fresh cilantro (optional)**

****Use a rotisserie chicken for best flavor and convenience.***

1. Preheat oven to 425°F. Roll out dough into 15-inch circle on lightly floured surface.
2. Brush oil over bottom and side of large (12-inch) cast iron skillet; place in oven 5 minutes to preheat.
3. Combine chicken and ½ cup barbecue sauce in medium bowl; toss to coat. Remove hot skillet from oven; press dough into bottom and about 1 inch up side of skillet.
4. Spread remaining ¼ cup barbecue sauce over dough. Sprinkle with mozzarella; top with chicken mixture. Sprinkle with half of onion and Gouda; top with remaining onion.
5. Bake 25 minutes or until crust is golden brown. Garnish with cilantro.

Makes 4 to 6 servings

CHICKEN SCARPIELLO

- 3 tablespoons extra virgin olive oil, divided
- 1 pound spicy Italian sausage, cut into 1-inch pieces
- 1 whole chicken (about 3 pounds), cut into 10 pieces*
- 1 teaspoon salt, divided
- 1 large onion, chopped
- 2 red, yellow or orange bell peppers, cut into ¼-inch strips
- 3 cloves garlic, minced
- ½ cup dry white wine (such as sauvignon blanc)
- ½ cup chicken broth
- ½ cup coarsely chopped seeded hot cherry peppers
- ½ cup liquid from cherry pepper jar
- 1 teaspoon dried oregano
- Additional salt and black pepper
- ¼ cup chopped fresh Italian parsley

**Or, purchase 2 bone-in chicken leg quarters and 2 chicken breasts; separate drumsticks and thighs and cut breasts in half.*

1. Heat 1 tablespoon oil in large cast iron skillet over medium-high heat. Add sausage; cook about 10 minutes or until well browned on all sides, stirring occasionally. Remove sausage to plate.
2. Heat 1 tablespoon oil in same skillet. Sprinkle chicken with ½ teaspoon salt; arrange skin side down in single layer in skillet (cook in batches, if necessary). Cook about 6 minutes per side or until browned. Remove chicken from skillet; set aside. Drain fat from skillet.
3. Heat remaining 1 tablespoon oil in skillet. Add onion and ½ teaspoon salt; cook and stir 2 minutes or until onion is softened, scraping up browned bits from bottom of skillet. Add bell peppers and garlic; cook and stir 5 minutes. Stir in wine; cook until liquid is reduced by half. Stir in broth, cherry peppers, cherry pepper liquid and oregano. Season with additional salt and black pepper; bring to a simmer.
4. Return sausage and chicken along with any accumulated juices to skillet. Partially cover skillet; cook 10 minutes. Uncover; cook 15 minutes or until chicken is cooked through (165°F). Sprinkle with parsley.

Makes 6 servings

TIP **If too much liquid remains in the skillet when the chicken is cooked through, remove the chicken and sausage and continue simmering the sauce to reduce it slightly.**

AUSSIE CHICKEN

- ½ cup honey
- ½ cup Dijon mustard
- 2 tablespoons vegetable oil, divided
- 1 teaspoon lemon juice
- 4 boneless skinless chicken breasts (about 6 ounces each)
- Salt and black pepper
- 1 tablespoon butter
- 2 cups sliced mushrooms
- 4 slices bacon, cooked
- ½ cup (2 ounces) shredded Cheddar cheese
- ½ cup (2 ounces) shredded Monterey Jack cheese
- Chopped fresh parsley

1. Whisk honey, mustard, 1 tablespoon oil and lemon juice in medium bowl until well blended. Reserve half of marinade mixture to use as sauce; cover and refrigerate until ready to serve.
2. Place chicken in large resealable food storage bag. Pour remaining half of marinade over chicken; seal bag and turn to coat. Refrigerate at least 2 hours.
3. Preheat oven to 375°F. Remove chicken from marinade; discard marinade. Heat remaining 1 tablespoon oil in large cast iron skillet over medium-high heat. Add chicken; cook 3 to 4 minutes per side or until golden brown. (Chicken will not be cooked through.) Remove to plate; sprinkle with salt and pepper.
4. Heat butter in same skillet over medium-high heat. Add mushrooms; cook 8 minutes or until mushrooms begin to brown, stirring occasionally and scraping up browned bits from bottom of skillet. Season with salt and pepper. Return chicken to skillet; spoon mushrooms over chicken. Top with bacon; sprinkle with Cheddar and Monterey Jack.
5. Bake 8 to 10 minutes or until chicken is cooked through (165°F) and cheese is melted. Sprinkle with parsley; serve with reserved honey-mustard mixture.

Makes 4 servings

QUICK MEXICAN SKILLET DINNER

- 1 tablespoon vegetable oil
- 12 ounces ground turkey
- 1 can (about 14 ounces) stewed tomatoes
- ½ (16-ounce) package frozen bell pepper stir-fry blend, thawed
- ¾ teaspoon ground cumin
- ½ teaspoon salt
- ½ cup (2 ounces) finely shredded sharp Cheddar cheese
- 2 ounces tortilla chips, lightly crushed

1. Heat oil in large cast iron skillet over medium heat. Add turkey; cook 5 minutes or until no longer pink, stirring to break up meat.
2. Stir in tomatoes, bell peppers, cumin and salt; bring to a boil. Reduce heat to low; cover and cook 20 minutes or until vegetables are tender. Sprinkle with cheese and chips.

Makes 4 servings

BLACKENED CHICKEN TORTA

- 2 tablespoons vegetable oil
- 1½ tablespoons Creole seasoning
- 4 boneless skinless chicken breasts (about 6 ounces each)
- ½ cup sour cream
- 2 teaspoons lime juice, divided
- ½ teaspoon ground cumin
- ¼ teaspoon salt, divided
- Dash black pepper
- ⅓ cup mayonnaise
- ½ teaspoon chipotle chili powder
- 1 ripe avocado
- 4 slices (about 1 ounce each) Cheddar cheese
- 4 slices (about 1 ounce each) pepper Jack cheese
- 4 ciabatta rolls, split
- 1 cup finely shredded green cabbage or coleslaw mix

1. Combine oil and Creole seasoning in shallow dish; mix well. Add chicken; turn to coat completely with spice mixture. Let stand while preparing sauces.
2. Combine sour cream, 1½ teaspoons lime juice, cumin, ⅛ teaspoon salt and dash of pepper in medium bowl; mix well. Combine mayonnaise, remaining ½ teaspoon lime juice, ⅛ teaspoon salt and chipotle chili powder in small bowl; mix well. Mash avocado in another small bowl; season with additional salt and pepper.
3. Heat large cast iron skillet over medium-high heat until very hot. Add chicken to hot skillet; cook about 6 minutes per side or until well browned and cooked through (165°F). Remove to plate; top each chicken breast with one slice Cheddar and one slice pepper Jack cheese. Tent loosely with foil to melt cheese.
4. For each sandwich, spread 2 tablespoons sour cream mixture on bottom half of roll; top with mashed avocado. Layer with ¼ cup cabbage and cheese-topped chicken breast. Spread heaping tablespoon mayonnaise mixture on top half of roll; close sandwich.

Makes 4 servings

CHICKEN SALTIMBOCCA

- 4 boneless skinless chicken breasts (about 6 ounces each)
- ¼ teaspoon salt
- 2 tablespoons chopped fresh sage
- 4 thin slices prosciutto
- 1 to 2 tablespoons all-purpose flour
- 2 tablespoons olive oil
- ⅓ cup dry white wine
- 1 can (about 14 ounces) quartered artichoke hearts, drained
- ¼ cup whipping cream
- 2 tablespoons butter, cut into pieces
- 2 tablespoons lemon juice
- 2 tablespoons capers, rinsed and drained
- Chopped fresh parsley (optional)

1. Pound chicken breasts to even thickness (about ½ inch thick) between two sheets of waxed paper or plastic wrap with meat mallet or rolling pin. Season both sides of chicken with salt. Sprinkle one side of each chicken breast with sage; top with prosciutto slice. Pound chicken again so prosciutto adheres to chicken and flattens slightly. (Chicken should be between ¼ and ½ inch thick.) Dust both sides lightly with flour.
2. Heat oil in large cast iron skillet over medium-high heat. Add chicken, prosciutto sides down; cook about 5 minutes per side or until browned and cooked through (165°F). Remove chicken to platter; tent with foil to keep warm. Drain excess fat from skillet if necessary.
3. Add wine to skillet; cook 2 minutes, scraping up browned bits from bottom of skillet. Add artichokes, cream, butter and lemon juice; cook about 4 minutes or until sauce thickens and artichokes are heated through.
4. Pour sauce over chicken; sprinkle with capers and parsley, if desired.

Makes 4 servings

CHICKEN AND AVOCADO OVERSTUFFED QUESADILLAS

- **3 tablespoons Caesar dressing**
- **2 teaspoons finely chopped fresh cilantro**
- **2 burrito-size flour tortillas (10 to 11 inches)**
- **¾ cup (3 ounces) grated Monterey Jack cheese, divided**
- **1 cup chopped grilled chicken strips (¾-inch pieces)**
- **½ cup shredded green cabbage**
- **½ cup pico de gallo**
- **1 avocado, sliced**
- **2 tablespoons vegetable oil**

1. Combine dressing and cilantro in small bowl; mix well. Roll up tortillas in paper towel or waxed paper; microwave on HIGH 10 seconds or until softened.
2. Place tortillas on work surface. For each quesadilla, sprinkle ¼ cup cheese in circle in center of tortilla, leaving 3-inch border all around. Top with half of chicken; drizzle with half of dressing mixture. Top with half each of cabbage, pico de gallo and avocado; sprinkle with 2 tablespoons cheese.
3. Working with one tortilla at a time, fold top of tortilla down over filling to center. Hold folded part down while working in clockwise direction, folding next section of tortilla in towards center until filling is completely covered. (You should end up with five folds and a hexagonal shape. If there is an uncovered hole in center of tortilla after folding, cut round piece from another tortilla to cover it.)
4. Heat 1 tablespoon oil in medium cast iron skillet over medium heat. Cook quesadilla, folded side down, about 5 minutes or until golden brown, pressing down with spatula. Turn and cook 4 to 5 minutes or until top is golden brown. Repeat with remaining 1 tablespoon oil and quesadilla.

Makes 2 servings

LEMON BUTTER CHICKEN

- 4 boneless skinless chicken breasts (about 6 ounces each)
- ½ teaspoon salt
- ¼ teaspoon black pepper
- 1 tablespoon olive oil
- 6 tablespoons (¾ stick) butter, divided
- ¼ cup finely chopped onion
- 2 cloves garlic, minced
- ½ cup dry white wine
- ¼ cup lemon juice
- 3 tablespoons thinly sliced oil-packed sun-dried tomatoes (about 4)
- 3 tablespoons slivered fresh basil
- 1 package (4 ounces) goat cheese, cut into 4 pieces

1. Pound chicken to ½-inch thickness between two sheets of waxed paper or plastic wrap with meat mallet or rolling pin. (Chicken may not need much flattening, but make sure all pieces are even thickness.) Season with salt and pepper.
2. Heat oil in large cast iron skillet over medium-high heat. Add chicken; cook 6 to 8 minutes per side or until lightly browned and no longer pink in center. Remove to plate; tent with foil to keep warm.
3. Add 1 tablespoon butter and onion to skillet; cook and stir 2 minutes or until softened. Add garlic; cook and stir 1 minute. Add wine and lemon juice; bring to a simmer. Cook 10 minutes or until reduced by half.
4. Add remaining 5 tablespoons butter, 1 tablespoon at a time, whisking until smooth. Stir in sun-dried tomatoes and basil; cook just until heated through.
5. Place chicken on serving plates; top with goat cheese and sauce.

Makes 4 servings

CHICKEN SAUSAGE AND TWO-GRAIN SKILLET CASSEROLE

1 tablespoon olive oil

1 package (12 ounces) fully-cooked chicken apple sausage links, cut into ½-inch slices

1 can (about 14 ounces) chicken broth

1 cup uncooked instant brown rice

½ cup uncooked quinoa

1 red bell pepper, cut into thin strips

1 stalk celery, diagonally sliced

1½ teaspoons curry powder *or* 1 teaspoon ground turmeric

½ cup thawed frozen peas

¼ cup finely chopped green onions (optional)

1. Heat oil in large cast iron skillet over medium-high heat. Add sausage; cook 4 minutes or until browned, stirring occasionally.
2. Stir in broth, rice, quinoa, bell pepper, celery and curry powder; bring to a boil. Reduce heat to low; cover and simmer 12 minutes or until liquid is absorbed.
3. Remove from heat; stir in peas. Let stand 5 minutes before serving. Sprinkle with green onions, if desired.

Makes 4 servings

DOUBLE DECKER TACOS

- 2 tablespoons all-purpose flour
- 2 teaspoons chili powder
- 1 teaspoon dried minced onion
- ¾ teaspoon paprika
- ½ teaspoon salt
- ½ teaspoon garlic powder
- ¼ teaspoon sugar
- 1 pound ground beef
- ⅔ cup water
- 8 taco shells
- 8 mini (5-inch) flour tortillas*
- 2 cups refried beans, warmed
- 1 cup shredded romaine lettuce
- 1 cup chopped tomato
- 1 cup (4 ounces) shredded Cheddar cheese
- Sour cream (optional)

**Mini flour tortillas may also be labeled as street tacos.*

1. Preheat oven to 350°F. Combine flour, chili powder, onion, paprika, salt, garlic powder and sugar in small bowl; mix well.
2. Cook beef in large cast iron skillet over medium-high heat 6 to 8 minutes or until browned, stirring to break up meat. Drain fat. Add flour mixture; cook and stir 2 minutes. Stir in water; bring to a simmer. Reduce heat to medium; cook 10 minutes or until most of liquid has evaporated.
3. Meanwhile, heat taco shells in oven 5 minutes or until warm.
4. Wrap tortillas in damp paper towel; microwave on HIGH 25 to 35 seconds or until warm. Spread each tortilla with ¼ cup refried beans, leaving ¼-inch border around edge. Wrap flour tortillas around outside of taco shells, pressing gently to seal together.
5. Fill taco shells with beef mixture; top with lettuce, tomato and cheese. Drizzle with sour cream, if desired. Serve immediately.

Makes 8 tacos

MONGOLIAN BEEF

- 1¼ pounds beef flank steak
- ¼ cup cornstarch
- 3 tablespoons vegetable oil, divided
- 3 cloves garlic, minced
- 2 teaspoons grated fresh ginger
- ½ cup water
- ½ cup soy sauce
- ⅓ cup packed dark brown sugar
- Pinch red pepper flakes
- 2 green onions, diagonally sliced into 1-inch pieces
- Hot cooked rice (optional)

1. Cut flank steak in half lengthwise, then cut crosswise against the grain into ¼-inch slices.
2. Combine beef and cornstarch in medium bowl; toss to coat.
3. Heat 1 tablespoon oil in large cast iron skillet over high heat. Add half of beef in single layer (do not crowd); cook 1 to 2 minutes per side or until browned. Remove to clean bowl. Repeat with remaining beef and 1 tablespoon oil.
4. Heat remaining 1 tablespoon oil in same skillet over medium heat. Add garlic and ginger; cook and stir 30 seconds. Add water, soy sauce, brown sugar and red pepper flakes; bring to a boil, stirring until well blended. Cook 8 minutes or until slightly thickened, stirring occasionally.
5. Return beef to skillet; cook 2 to 3 minutes or until sauce thickens and beef is heated through. Stir in green onions. Serve with rice, if desired.

Makes 4 servings

SAUSAGE AND BEAN STEW

2 cups fresh bread crumbs*
2 tablespoons olive oil, divided
1 pound uncooked pork sausage, cut into 2-inch pieces
1 leek, white and light green parts only, cut in half and thinly sliced
1 large onion, cut into quarters and cut into ¼-inch slices
1 teaspoon salt, divided
2 cloves garlic, minced
½ teaspoon dried thyme
½ teaspoon ground sage
¼ teaspoon paprika
¼ teaspoon ground allspice
¼ teaspoon black pepper
1 can (28 ounces) diced tomatoes
2 cans (about 15 ounces each) navy or cannellini beans, rinsed and drained
2 tablespoons whole grain mustard
Fresh thyme leaves (optional)

To make bread crumbs, cut 4 ounces stale baguette or country bread into several pieces; place in food processor. Pulse until coarse crumbs form.

1. Preheat oven to 350°F. Combine bread crumbs and 1 tablespoon oil in medium bowl; mix well.
2. Heat remaining 1 tablespoon oil in large cast iron skillet over medium-high heat. Add sausage; cook 8 minutes or until browned, stirring occasionally. (Sausage will not be cooked through.) Remove to plate.
3. Add leek, onion and ½ teaspoon salt to skillet; cook 10 minutes or until vegetables are soft and beginning to brown, stirring occasionally. Add garlic; cook and stir 1 minute. Add dried thyme, sage, paprika, allspice and pepper; cook and stir 1 minute. Add tomatoes; cook 5 minutes, stirring occasionally. Stir in beans, mustard and remaining ½ teaspoon salt; bring to a simmer.
4. Return sausage to skillet, pushing down into bean mixture. Sprinkle with bread crumbs.
5. Bake 25 minutes or until bread crumbs are lightly browned and sausage is cooked through. Garnish with fresh thyme.

Makes 4 to 6 servings

STEAK FAJITAS

- ¼ cup lime juice
- ¼ cup soy sauce
- 4 tablespoons vegetable oil, divided
- 2 tablespoons honey
- 2 tablespoons Worcestershire sauce
- 2 cloves garlic, minced
- ½ teaspoon ground red pepper
- 1 pound flank steak, skirt steak or top sirloin
- 1 medium yellow onion, halved and cut into ¼-inch slices
- 1 green bell pepper, cut into ¼-inch strips
- 1 red bell pepper, cut into ¼-inch strips
- Flour tortillas, warmed
- Lime wedges (optional)
- Optional toppings: pico de gallo, guacamole, sour cream, shredded lettuce and shredded Cheddar-Jack cheese

1. Combine lime juice, soy sauce, 2 tablespoons oil, honey, Worcestershire sauce, garlic and ground red pepper in medium bowl; mix well. Remove ¼ cup marinade to large bowl.
2. Place steak in large resealable food storage bag. Pour remaining marinade over steak; seal bag and turn to coat. Marinate in refrigerator at least 2 hours or overnight. Add onion and bell peppers to bowl with ¼ cup marinade; toss to coat. Cover and refrigerate until ready to use.
3. Remove steak from marinade; discard marinade and pat steak dry with paper towels. Heat 1 tablespoon oil in large cast iron skillet over medium-high heat. Cook steak 4 minutes per side for medium rare or to desired doneness. Remove to large cutting board; tent with foil and let stand 10 minutes.
4. Meanwhile, heat remaining 1 tablespoon oil in same skillet over medium-high heat. Add vegetable mixture; cook 8 minutes or until vegetables are crisp-tender and beginning to brown in spots, stirring occasionally. (Cook in two batches if necessary; do not crowd vegetables in skillet.)
5. Cut steak into thin slices across the grain. Serve with vegetables, tortillas, lime wedges and desired toppings.

Makes 2 servings

HAM AND BARBECUED BEAN SKILLET

- 1 tablespoon vegetable oil
- 1 cup chopped onion
- 1 teaspoon minced garlic
- 1 can (about 15 ounces) kidney beans, rinsed and drained
- 1 can (about 15 ounces) cannellini or Great Northern beans, rinsed and drained
- 1 cup chopped green bell pepper
- ½ cup packed brown sugar
- ½ cup ketchup
- 2 tablespoons cider vinegar
- 2 teaspoons dry mustard
- 1 ham steak (½ inch thick, about 12 ounces)

1. Heat oil in large cast iron skillet over medium-high heat. Add onion and garlic; cook and stir 3 minutes. Add beans, bell pepper, brown sugar, ketchup, vinegar and mustard; mix well.
2. Trim fat from ham; cut ham into ½-inch pieces.
3. Add ham to skillet. Reduce heat to low; cook 5 minutes or until sauce thickens and mixture is heated through, stirring occasionally.

Makes 4 servings

CLASSIC PATTY MELTS

- 5 tablespoons butter, divided
- 2 large yellow onions, thinly sliced
- ¾ teaspoon plus pinch salt, divided
- 1 pound ground chuck (80% lean)
- ½ teaspoon garlic powder
- ½ teaspoon onion powder
- ¼ teaspoon black pepper
- 8 slices marble rye bread
- ½ cup Thousand Island dressing
- 8 slices (about 1 ounce each) deli American or Swiss cheese

1. Melt 2 tablespoons butter in large cast iron skillet over medium heat. Add onions and pinch of salt; cook 20 minutes or until onions are very soft and golden brown, stirring occasionally. Remove to small bowl; wipe out skillet.
2. Combine beef, remaining ¾ teaspoon salt, garlic powder, onion powder and pepper in medium bowl; mix gently. Shape into four patties about the size and shape of bread slices and ¼ to ½ inch thick.
3. Melt 1 tablespoon butter in same skillet over medium-high heat. Add patties, two at a time; cook 3 minutes or until bottoms are browned, pressing down gently with spatula to form crust. Turn patties; cook 3 minutes or until browned. Remove patties to plate; wipe out skillet with paper towel.
4. Spread one side of each bread slice with dressing. Top four bread slices with cheese slice, patty, caramelized onions, another cheese slice and remaining bread slices.
5. Melt 1 tablespoon butter in same skillet over medium heat. Add two sandwiches to skillet; cook 4 minutes or until golden brown, pressing down with spatula to crisp bread. Turn sandwiches; cook 4 minutes or until golden brown and cheese is melted. Repeat with remaining 1 tablespoon butter and sandwiches.

Makes 4 servings

PORK WITH SPICY ORANGE CRANBERRY SAUCE

- 1 teaspoon chili powder
- ½ teaspoon ground cumin
- ¼ teaspoon ground allspice
- ¼ teaspoon salt
- ¼ teaspoon black pepper
- 4 boneless pork chops (about 1 pound)
- 1 tablespoon canola oil
- 1 cup whole-berry cranberry sauce
- ½ teaspoon grated orange peel
- ¼ teaspoon ground cinnamon
- ⅛ teaspoon red pepper flakes

1. Combine chili powder, cumin, allspice, salt and black pepper in small bowl; mix well. Sprinkle evenly over both sides of pork chops.
2. Heat oil in large cast iron skillet over medium heat. Add pork; cook 4 to 5 minutes per side or until barely pink in center.
3. Meanwhile, combine cranberry sauce, orange peel, cinnamon and red pepper flakes in small bowl; mix well. Serve sauce with pork chops.

Makes 4 servings

RENEGADE STEAK

- **1½ teaspoons coarse salt**
- **½ teaspoon paprika**
- **½ teaspoon black pepper**
- **¼ teaspoon onion powder**
- **¼ teaspoon garlic powder**
- **⅛ teaspoon ground turmeric**
- **⅛ teaspoon ground red pepper**
- **⅛ teaspoon ground coriander**
- **2 center-cut sirloin, strip or tri-tip steaks (about 8 ounces each)**
- **2 tablespoons vegetable oil**
- **1 tablespoon butter**

1. Combine salt, paprika, black pepper, onion powder, garlic powder, turmeric, red pepper and coriander in small bowl; mix well.
2. Season both sides of steaks with spice mixture (you will not need all of it); let steaks stand at room temperature 45 minutes before cooking.
3. Heat large cast iron skillet over high heat. Add oil; heat until oil shimmers and just begins to smoke. Add steaks to skillet; cook 30 seconds, then turn steaks. Cook 30 seconds, then turn again. Continue cooking and turning every 30 seconds for 4 minutes or until golden brown crust begins to form.
4. Add butter to skillet; continue cooking and turning every 30 seconds for 1 minute or until steaks reach 130° to 135°F for medium rare or 140° to 145°F for medium.* Remove to plate; let steaks rest 5 minutes before serving.

**Timing given is approximate for 1½-inch steaks; thinner steaks will take less time to cook.*

Makes 2 servings

SAUSAGE AND PEPPERS

- 1 pound uncooked hot or mild Italian sausage links
- 2 tablespoons olive oil
- 3 medium onions, cut into ½-inch slices
- 2 red bell peppers, cut into ½-inch slices
- 2 green bell peppers, cut into ½-inch slices
- 1½ teaspoons coarse salt, divided
- 1 teaspoon dried oregano
- Italian rolls (optional)

1. Fill medium saucepan half full with water or beer; bring to a boil over high heat. Add sausage; cook 5 minutes over medium heat. Drain and cut diagonally into 1-inch slices.
2. Heat oil in large cast iron skillet over medium-high heat. Add sausage; cook about 10 minutes or until browned, stirring occasionally. Remove sausage to plate.
3. Add onions, bell peppers, 1 teaspoon salt and oregano to skillet; cook over medium heat about 25 minutes or until vegetables are very soft and browned in spots, stirring occasionally.
4. Stir sausage and remaining ½ teaspoon salt into skillet; cook 3 minutes or until heated through. Serve with rolls, if desired.

Makes 4 servings

SMASHED BACON BURGER

4 slices bacon, cut in half
1 pound ground beef
Salt and black pepper
4 slices (about 1 ounce each) sharp Cheddar cheese
4 eggs (optional)
Lettuce leaves
4 brioche rolls or hamburger buns

1. Cook bacon in large cast iron skillet over medium-high heat until crisp. Drain on paper towel-lined plate. Drain all but 1 tablespoon drippings from skillet.
2. Divide beef into four portions; shape lightly into loose balls. Place in same skillet over medium-high heat. Smash with spatula to flatten into thin patties; sprinkle with salt and pepper. Cook 2 to 3 minutes or until edges and bottoms are browned.
3. Turn burgers; top with cheese. Cook 2 to 3 minutes for medium rare or to desired doneness. Remove to plates.
4. If desired, crack eggs into hot skillet. Cook over medium heat 3 minutes or until whites are opaque and yolks reach desired degree of doneness, turning once, if desired, for over easy.
5. Place lettuce leaves and burgers on rolls; top with eggs and bacon.

Makes 4 servings

CHINESE PEPPERCORN BEEF

- 2 teaspoons whole black and pink peppercorns*
- 2 teaspoons coriander seeds
- 1 tablespoon peanut or canola oil
- 1 boneless beef top sirloin steak, about 1¼ inches thick (1¼ to 1½ pounds)
- 2 teaspoons dark sesame oil
- ½ cup thinly sliced shallots or sweet onion
- ½ cup chicken broth
- 2 tablespoons soy sauce
- 1 tablespoon dry sherry
- 1 tablespoon cold water
- 1 teaspoon cornstarch
- 2 tablespoons thinly sliced green onion or chopped fresh cilantro

**Or use all black peppercorns if preferred.*

1. Place peppercorns and coriander seeds in small resealable food storage bag; seal bag. Coarsely crush spices using meat mallet or bottom of heavy saucepan.
2. Brush peanut oil over both sides of steak; sprinkle with peppercorn mixture, pressing lightly.
3. Heat large cast iron skillet over medium-high heat. Add steak; cook 4 minutes without moving or until seared on bottom. Reduce heat to medium; turn steak and cook 3 to 4 minutes for medium rare or to desired doneness. Remove steak to cutting board; tent with foil and let stand while preparing sauce.
4. Add sesame oil to same skillet; heat over medium heat. Add shallots; cook 3 minutes, stirring frequently. Add broth, soy sauce and sherry; cook 2 minutes.
5. Stir water into cornstarch in small bowl until smooth. Add to skillet; cook and stir 3 to 4 minutes or until sauce thickens.
6. Cut steak crosswise into thin slices. Spoon sauce over steak; sprinkle with green onion.

Makes 4 servings

PIZZA CASSEROLE

- 2 cups uncooked rotini or other spiral pasta
- 1½ pounds ground beef
- 1 medium onion, chopped
- Salt and black pepper
- 1 can (about 15 ounces) pizza sauce
- 1 can (8 ounces) tomato sauce
- 1 can (6 ounces) tomato paste
- ½ teaspoon sugar
- ½ teaspoon garlic salt
- ½ teaspoon dried oregano
- 2 cups (8 ounces) shredded mozzarella cheese
- 12 to 15 slices pepperoni

1. Preheat oven to 350°F. Cook pasta according to package directions until al dente; drain.
2. Meanwhile, brown beef and onion in large cast iron skillet over medium-high heat 6 to 8 minutes, stirring to break up meat. Drain fat. Season with salt and pepper.
3. Combine pasta, pizza sauce, tomato sauce, tomato paste, sugar, garlic salt and oregano in large bowl; mix well. Add beef mixture; stir until blended.
4. Spread half of mixture in same skillet; top with 1 cup cheese. Repeat layers of pasta mixture and cheese; top with pepperoni.
5. Bake 25 to 30 minutes or until heated through and cheese is melted.

Makes 6 servings

PORK SCALOPPINE

- ⅓ cup all-purpose flour
- ¾ teaspoon salt
- ½ teaspoon black pepper
- 1 pound pork tenderloin, cut into ½-inch-thick slices
- 3 tablespoons olive oil, divided
- 16 ounces sliced mushrooms
- ½ cup sliced green onions
- ½ cup water
- ¼ cup dry white wine
- ½ teaspoon dried marjoram
- ½ teaspoon dried basil
- ½ cup chopped pimiento-stuffed green olives (optional)
- Hot cooked orzo pasta or rice

1. Combine flour, salt and pepper in shallow bowl; mix well. Pound pork slices to ¼-inch thickness with meat mallet or rolling pin. Coat with flour mixture; shake off excess.
2. Heat 1 tablespoon oil in large cast iron skillet over medium-high heat. Add mushrooms; cook and stir 6 to 8 minutes or until tender. Remove to medium bowl; cover to keep warm.
3. Heat remaining 2 tablespoons oil in same skillet. Add pork; cook 1 to 2 minutes per side or until browned. Add green onions, water, wine, marjoram and basil; bring to a simmer. Stir in olives, if desired; cover and cook 3 to 4 minutes per side or until pork is barely pink in center. Remove pork to serving platter.
4. Return mushrooms with any accumulated juices to skillet; cook 2 to 3 minutes or until heated through. Serve pork with sauce and orzo.

Makes 4 to 6 servings

SEAFOOD

SPANISH-STYLE PAELLA

- 6 cups chicken broth
- 3 tablespoons olive oil
- 8 ounces boneless skinless chicken thighs, cut into bite-size pieces
- 2 to 3 links Spanish chorizo sausage (about 5 ounces), sliced
- 1 medium onion, chopped
- 1 red bell pepper, chopped
- 4 cloves garlic, minced
- 1 teaspoon crushed saffron threads
- 1½ cups uncooked rice
- 1 can (10 ounces) diced tomatoes with chiles
- 3 tablespoons tomato paste
- ½ teaspoon salt
- ¼ teaspoon black pepper
- 1 pound large raw shrimp, peeled and deveined (with tails on)
- 8 ounces mussels, scrubbed and debearded
- ½ cup frozen peas, thawed

1. Heat broth to a boil in medium saucepan over high heat. Reduce heat to low to keep warm.
2. Heat oil in large cast iron skillet over medium-high heat. Add chicken and chorizo; cook 1 minute, stirring once. Add onion, bell pepper, garlic and saffron; cook and stir 5 minutes or until chorizo is browned and vegetables are softened.
3. Add rice, tomatoes, tomato paste, salt and black pepper; cook 5 minutes, stirring occasionally. Add broth, ½ to 1 cup at a time, stirring after each addition until broth is almost absorbed.
4. Cover skillet with foil or lid; cook over medium heat 25 to 30 minutes or until rice is tender.
5. Remove foil; gently stir in shrimp, mussels and peas. Replace foil; cook 5 to 10 minutes or until shrimp are pink and opaque and mussels open. Discard any unopened mussels.

Makes 8 servings

ISLAND FISH TACOS

COLESLAW

- 1 medium jicama, peeled and shredded
- 2 cups packaged coleslaw mix
- 3 tablespoons finely chopped fresh cilantro
- ¼ cup lime juice
- ¼ cup vegetable oil
- 3 tablespoons white vinegar
- 2 tablespoons mayonnaise
- 1 tablespoon honey
- 1 teaspoon salt

SALSA

- 2 medium fresh tomatoes, diced (about 2 cups)
- ½ cup finely chopped red onion
- ¼ cup finely chopped fresh cilantro
- 2 tablespoons lime juice
- 2 tablespoons minced jalapeño pepper
- 1 teaspoon salt

TACOS

- 1 to 1¼ pounds white fish such as tilapia or mahi mahi, cut into 3×1½-inch pieces
- Salt and black pepper
- 2 tablespoons vegetable oil
- 12 (6-inch) tortillas, heated
- Guacamole (optional)

1. For coleslaw, combine jicama, coleslaw mix and 3 tablespoons cilantro in medium bowl; mix well. Whisk ¼ cup lime juice, ¼ cup oil, vinegar, mayonnaise, honey and 1 teaspoon salt in small bowl until well blended. Pour over vegetable mixture; stir to coat. Let stand at least 15 minutes for flavors to blend.
2. For salsa, place tomatoes in fine-mesh strainer; set in bowl or sink to drain 15 minutes. Remove to another medium bowl. Stir in onion, ¼ cup cilantro, 2 tablespoons lime juice, jalapeño and 1 teaspoon salt; mix well.
3. For tacos, season both sides of fish with salt and black pepper. Heat 1 tablespoon oil in large cast iron skillet over medium-high heat. Add half of fish; cook 2 minutes per side or until fish is opaque and begins to flake when tested with fork. Repeat with remaining oil and fish.
4. Break fish into bite-size pieces; serve in tortillas with coleslaw, salsa and guacamole, if desired.

Makes 4 servings

CRUNCHY SALMON PATTIES

- 1 package (3 ounces) Asian-flavored ramen noodles
- ¼ cup all-purpose flour
- 2 cans (6 ounces each) pink salmon, drained and flaked
- ¼ cup finely chopped onion
- ¼ cup finely chopped red bell pepper
- 2 eggs, lightly beaten
- 2 tablespoons vegetable oil

1. Combine ramen noodles, flour and seasoning packet in food processor; process until noodles are finely chopped.
2. Combine salmon, onion, bell pepper and half of noodle mixture in large bowl; mix well. Add eggs; stir until blended.
3. Place remaining noodle mixture on large plate. Shape salmon mixture into eight patties. Press both sides of patties into noodle mixture to coat.
4. Heat oil in large cast iron skillet over medium-high heat. Cook patties in batches 3 to 5 minutes per side or until golden brown.

Makes 8 patties

TIP **Serve salmon patties with tartar sauce, sweet and sour sauce or spicy mustard.**

PAN-ROASTED PIKE WITH BUTTERY BREAD CRUMBS

- 6 tablespoons (¾ stick) butter, divided
- 2 cloves garlic, minced
- ⅓ cup plain dry bread crumbs
- ½ teaspoon salt, divided
- 4 tablespoons chopped fresh parsley
- 4 pike fillets or other medium-firm white fish (about 6 ounces each)
- ⅛ teaspoon black pepper
- 2 tablespoons lemon juice
- Fresh parsley leaves (optional)

1. Preheat oven to 400°F.
2. Melt 2 tablespoons butter in small nonstick skillet over medium-high heat. Add garlic; cook and stir 1 minute or just until lightly browned. Add bread crumbs and ⅛ teaspoon salt; cook and stir 1 minute. Transfer to small bowl; stir in chopped parsley.
3. Melt 1 tablespoon butter in large cast iron skillet over medium-high heat. Sprinkle fish with ¼ teaspoon salt and pepper. Add to skillet, flesh side down; cook 1 minute.
4. Remove from heat; turn fish and top with bread crumb mixture. Transfer to oven; roast 8 to 10 minutes or until fish begins to flake when tested with fork.
5. Wipe out small skillet with paper towel; heat over medium heat. Add remaining 3 tablespoons butter; cook 3 to 4 minutes or until melted and lightly browned, stirring occasionally. Stir in lemon juice and remaining ⅛ teaspoon salt. Spoon over fish just before serving. Garnish with parsley leaves.

Makes 4 servings

BLACKENED SHRIMP WITH TOMATOES

- 1½ teaspoons paprika
- 1 teaspoon Italian seasoning
- ½ teaspoon salt
- ½ teaspoon garlic powder
- ¼ teaspoon black pepper
- 8 ounces small raw shrimp (about 24), peeled (with tails on)
- 1 tablespoon canola oil
- 1½ cups halved grape tomatoes
- ½ cup sliced onion, separated into rings
- Lime wedges (optional)

1. Combine paprika, Italian seasoning, salt, garlic powder and pepper in large resealable food storage bag; mix well. Add shrimp; seal bag and shake to coat.
2. Heat oil in large cast iron skillet over medium-high heat. Add shrimp; cook 4 minutes or until shrimp are pink and opaque, turning occasionally.
3. Add tomatoes and onion to skillet; cook 1 minute or until tomatoes are heated through and onion is softened. Serve with lime wedges, if desired.

Makes 2 to 3 servings

SOUTHWESTERN TILAPIA WITH RICE AND BEANS

- **2 tablespoons all-purpose flour**
- **½ teaspoon salt, divided**
- **⅛ teaspoon black pepper**
- **4 tilapia fillets (about 4 ounces each), patted dry**
- **2 tablespoons butter, divided**
- **1 can (about 15 ounces) black beans, rinsed and drained**
- **1 can (about 14 ounces) diced tomatoes with chiles**
- **1 package (about 8 ounces) ready-to-serve Spanish rice**
- **¼ teaspoon dried oregano**
- **1 green onion, finely chopped**

1. Combine flour, ¼ teaspoon salt and pepper in large resealable food storage bag; mix well. Add tilapia; seal bag and shake to coat.
2. Melt 1 tablespoon butter in large cast iron skillet over medium-high heat. Add fish; cook 2 minutes per side or until golden brown and fish begins to flake when tested with fork. Remove to plate; tent with foil to keep warm.
3. Melt remaining 1 tablespoon butter in same skillet. Stir in beans, tomatoes, rice, oregano and remaining ¼ teaspoon salt. Reduce heat to low; cook 5 minutes, stirring frequently.
4. Arrange fish over rice mixture. Sprinkle with green onion.

Makes 4 servings

SEARED SCALLOPS OVER GARLIC-LEMON SPINACH

- **1 tablespoon olive oil**
- **1 pound sea scallops* (about 12)**
- **¼ teaspoon salt**
- **⅛ teaspoon black pepper**
- **2 cloves garlic, minced**
- **1 shallot, minced**
- **1 package (about 6 ounces) baby spinach**
- **1 tablespoon lemon juice**
- **Lemon wedges (optional)**

***Make sure scallops are dry before adding them to the skillet so they can get a golden crust.*

1. Heat oil in large cast iron skillet over medium-high heat. Add scallops; sprinkle with salt and pepper. Cook 2 to 3 minutes per side or until golden brown. Remove to plate; keep warm.
2. Add garlic and shallot to skillet; cook and stir 45 seconds or until fragrant. Add spinach; cook 2 minutes or just until spinach begins to wilt, stirring occasionally. Remove from heat; stir in lemon juice.
3. Serve scallops over spinach. Garnish with lemon wedges.

Makes 3 to 4 servings

SALMON BLACK BEAN BURGERS

- 1 can (7½ ounces) pink salmon, drained
- ½ cup canned black beans, rinsed and drained
- ¼ cup plain dry bread crumbs
- ¼ cup sliced green onions
- 1 egg white
- 1 tablespoon chopped fresh cilantro
- 1 tablespoon lime juice
- ¼ teaspoon salt
- Pinch ground red pepper or seafood seasoning mix
- Black pepper
- 1 tablespoon canola oil

1. Place salmon in medium bowl; flake with fork.
2. Add beans, bread crumbs, green onions, egg white, cilantro, lime juice, salt and red pepper to salmon; mix well. Season with black pepper.
3. Shape mixture into three patties about 1¼ inches thick. Refrigerate 30 minutes or until ready to cook.
4. Heat oil in large cast iron skillet over medium heat. Add patties; cook 2 to 3 minutes per side or until golden brown.

Makes 3 servings

SERVING SUGGESTION Serve with whole grain hamburger buns and your favorite salsa.

PROSCIUTTO-WRAPPED SNAPPER

- **2 tablespoons olive oil, divided**
- **2 cloves garlic, minced**
- **4 skinless red snapper or halibut fillets (6 to 7 ounces each)**
- **½ teaspoon salt**
- **½ teaspoon black pepper**
- **8 large fresh sage leaves**
- **8 thin slices prosciutto (4 ounces total)**
- **¼ cup dry Marsala wine**

1. Preheat oven to 400°F. Combine 1 tablespoon oil and garlic in small bowl; brush over snapper. Sprinkle with salt and pepper.
2. Place 2 sage leaves on each fillet. Wrap 2 slices prosciutto around fish to enclose sage leaves; tuck in ends of prosciutto.
3. Heat remaining 1 tablespoon oil in large cast iron skillet over medium-high heat. Add fish, sage side down; cook 3 to 4 minutes or until prosciutto is crisp. Carefully turn fish; place skillet in oven.
4. Bake 8 to 10 minutes or until fish is opaque in center. Remove fish to serving plates; keep warm.
5. Pour wine into skillet; cook over medium-high heat 2 to 3 minutes or until liquid has reduced by half, stirring constantly and scraping up browned bits from bottom of skillet. Drizzle sauce over fish.

Makes 4 servings

ALMOND-COATED SCALLOPS

- 2½ tablespoons olive oil, divided
- 1 clove garlic, crushed
- ¼ cup coarse plain dry bread crumbs
- 2 tablespoons sliced almonds, chopped
- 1½ teaspoons grated lemon peel, divided
- ½ teaspoon salt
- ⅛ teaspoon black pepper
- 8 jumbo sea scallops (about 1 pound), cut in half horizontally

1. Heat 2 tablespoons oil in medium cast iron skillet over low heat. Add garlic; cook and stir 2 minutes. Remove from heat; discard garlic.
2. Combine bread crumbs, almonds, 1 teaspoon lemon peel, salt and pepper on plate; mix well.
3. Brush scallop slices with remaining ½ tablespoon oil; press scallops into bread crumb mixture to coat both sides.
4. Reheat oil in skillet over medium-high heat. Cook scallops in batches 2 to 3 minutes or until golden brown. Turn and cook 1 to 2 minutes. Sprinkle with remaining ½ teaspoon lemon peel. Serve immediately.

Makes 4 servings

LEMON SHRIMP WITH BLACK BEANS AND RICE

- 1 cup uncooked instant brown rice
- ⅛ teaspoon ground turmeric
- 3 tablespoons olive oil, divided
- 1 pound raw shrimp, peeled and deveined (with tails on)
- 1½ teaspoons chili powder
- ½ (15-ounce) can black beans, rinsed and drained
- 1 medium poblano pepper *or* ½ green bell pepper, minced
- 3 tablespoons lemon juice
- 2 teaspoons grated lemon peel
- ¾ teaspoon salt
- Lemon wedges (optional)

1. Cook rice with turmeric according to package directions.
2. Heat 1 tablespoon oil in large cast iron skillet over medium heat. Add shrimp and chili powder; cook and stir 4 minutes or until shrimp are pink and opaque.
3. Add remaining 2 tablespoons oil, beans, poblano pepper, lemon juice, lemon peel and salt; cook and stir 1 minute or until heated through.
4. Spoon shrimp mixture over rice. Garnish with lemon wedges.

Makes 4 servings

FRIED CATFISH WITH CHERRY SALSA

CHERRY SALSA

- 1 cup halved pitted fresh sweet cherries
- ¼ cup minced red onion
- 1 jalapeño pepper, seeded and minced
- 1 teaspoon balsamic vinegar
- ½ teaspoon salt
- Pinch ground allspice

FRIED CATFISH

- ¼ cup all-purpose flour
- 2 tablespoons cornmeal
- ¼ teaspoon salt
- ¼ teaspoon black pepper
- ¼ teaspoon paprika
- ⅛ teaspoon garlic salt
- 4 medium catfish fillets (about 1¼ pounds)
- 2 tablespoons vegetable oil
- Lime wedges
- Chopped fresh cilantro (optional)

1. For salsa, combine cherries, onion, jalapeño, vinegar, ½ teaspoon salt and allspice in small bowl; mix well.
2. For fish, combine flour, cornmeal, ¼ teaspoon salt, pepper, paprika and garlic salt in shallow bowl; mix well. Coat both sides of catfish with flour mixture.
3. Heat oil in large cast iron skillet over medium-high heat. Add fish; cook 4 to 5 minutes per side or until golden brown and opaque in center. Serve with salsa and lime wedges. Garnish with cilantro.

Makes 4 servings

VEGETARIAN ENTRÉES

VEGETABLE QUINOA FRITTATA

- 1 tablespoon olive oil
- 1 cup diced onion
- 1 cup small broccoli florets
- ¾ cup finely chopped red bell pepper
- 2 cloves garlic, minced
- 1 teaspoon salt
- ¼ teaspoon black pepper
- 1½ cups cooked quinoa
- ¼ cup sun-dried tomatoes, chopped
- 8 eggs, lightly beaten
- ¼ cup grated Parmesan cheese

1. Preheat oven to 400°F.
2. Heat oil in large cast iron skillet over medium-high heat. Add onion and broccoli; cook and stir 4 minutes. Add bell pepper; cook and stir 2 minutes. Add garlic, salt and black pepper; cook 30 seconds, stirring constantly. Stir in quinoa and sun-dried tomatoes.
3. Gently stir in eggs; cook until softly scrambled. Sprinkle with cheese.
4. Bake 7 minutes or until eggs are set. Let stand 5 minutes before cutting into wedges.

Makes 6 servings

BROCCOLI RAMEN FRITTERS WITH YOGURT DIPPING SAUCE

FRITTERS

- 2 eggs
- ¼ cup all-purpose flour
- 1 package (3 ounces) ramen noodles, any flavor, cooked 1 minute and coarsely chopped
- 2 cups steamed broccoli, finely chopped
- 2 tablespoons vegetable oil

YOGURT DIPPING SAUCE

- ½ cup plain Greek yogurt
- 1 tablespoon lime juice
- 2 teaspoons olive oil
- ¼ teaspoon salt

1. For fritters, whisk eggs, flour and ramen seasoning packet in medium bowl until well blended. Add chopped noodles and broccoli; mix well.
2. Heat 1 tablespoon vegetable oil in large cast iron skillet over medium-high heat. Drop broccoli mixture by ¼ cupfuls into skillet, being careful not to crowd pan. Cook 4 minutes; turn fritters and cook 3 minutes. Remove to plate; keep warm. Repeat with remaining vegetable oil and batter.
3. For sauce, combine yogurt, lime juice, olive oil and salt in small bowl; mix well. Serve with warm fritters.

Makes 8 fritters

SESAME GINGER TOFU BAHN MI

- 1 tablespoon sugar
- ¾ cup unseasoned rice vinegar
- 1 teaspoon salt
- 1 large carrot, spiraled or cut into julienne strips
- 4 ounces peeled daikon radish *or* 5 medium red radishes, spiraled or cut into julienne strips
- 1 (1-inch) piece peeled fresh ginger
- 1 clove garlic
- ¼ cup soy sauce
- 1 tablespoon packed brown sugar
- 1 tablespoon dark sesame oil
- 1 package (14 ounces) extra firm tofu, drained, pressed and halved crosswise
- 1 tablespoon vegetable oil
- 1 large loaf (16 ounces) *or* 2 small loaves (8 ounces each) soft French bread
- ¼ cup mayonnaise
- Fresh cilantro sprigs
- 8 ounces seedless cucumber (about 8 inches), cut into julienne strips
- 1 jalapeño pepper, thinly sliced into rings

1. Dissolve sugar in vinegar in 2-cup measuring cup; stir in salt. Measure 1 cup total of carrot and radish; add to vinegar mixture. Let stand at least 1 hour for flavors to blend.
2. Combine ginger and garlic in food processor; process until finely chopped. Add soy sauce, brown sugar and sesame oil; process until smooth. Place tofu in 8-inch square baking dish; pour marinade over tofu. Marinate at room temperature 30 minutes to 1 hour, turning occasionally.
3. Drain tofu, discarding marinade. Heat vegetable oil in large cast iron skillet over high heat. Add tofu in batches; cook 3 to 4 minutes per side or until well browned. Transfer to paper towel-lined cutting board; let stand until cool enough to handle. Cut into thin slices.
4. Scoop out some of soft insides of bread. Spread mayonnaise over bottom half of bread; top with tofu, cilantro, cucumber, carrot mixture and jalapeños.

Makes 4 to 8 servings

ASIAN NOODLE SKILLET

- 4 ounces soba (buckwheat) noodles
- 2 tablespoons vegetable oil, divided
- 1 package (16 ounces) firm tofu, cut into 1-inch cubes
- 4 cloves garlic, minced
- 1 tablespoon minced fresh ginger
- 1 can (8 ounces) water chestnuts
- 1 cup baby corn
- 1½ cups mushroom or vegetable broth
- 2 tablespoons soy sauce
- 1 cup snow peas
- ¼ cup green onions, thinly sliced

1. Bring about 6 cups water to boil in large saucepan over medium-high heat. Add noodles; boil 1 minute or until wilted. Rinse under cold water and drain.
2. Heat 1 tablespoon oil in large cast iron skillet over medium-high heat. Add tofu; cook until browned on all sides. Remove to plate.
3. Add remaining 1 tablespoon oil to skillet. Add garlic and ginger; cook and stir about 30 seconds or until fragrant. Stir in water chestnuts and corn.
4. Return browned tofu to skillet. Add broth, soy sauce, snow peas and drained noodles; bring to a boil. Reduce heat to low; cook 3 minutes or until noodles are cooked through and most of liquid has evaporated. Stir in green onions.

Makes 4 servings

QUINOA PATTIES WITH ROASTED RED PEPPER SAUCE

- 1 cup uncooked quinoa
- 2 cups water
- 1 jar (12 ounces) roasted red peppers, drained
- 1 tablespoon balsamic vinegar
- 1 teaspoon lemon juice
- 1 teaspoon sugar
- 1 clove garlic
- 4 eggs, beaten
- 1 cup Italian-seasoned dry bread crumbs
- ⅓ cup grated Parmesan cheese
- 2 tablespoons chopped fresh parsley
- 2 cloves garlic, minced
- ½ teaspoon salt
- 1 to 2 tablespoons olive oil

1. Place quinoa in fine-mesh strainer; rinse well under cold water.
2. Bring 2 cups water to a boil in medium saucepan over high heat; stir in quinoa. Reduce heat to low; cover and simmer 10 to 15 minutes or until quinoa is tender and water is absorbed. Cool slightly.
3. Meanwhile, combine roasted peppers, vinegar, lemon juice, sugar and garlic clove in blender or food processor; blend until smooth. Set aside.
4. Combine quinoa, eggs, bread crumbs, cheese, parsley, minced garlic and salt in large bowl; mix well. Shape into 12 (¼-cup) patties.
5. Heat 1 tablespoon oil in large cast iron skillet over medium heat. Add six patties; cook 5 to 7 minutes or until bottoms are browned. Turn and cook 5 to 7 minutes or until browned. Repeat with remaining patties, adding additional 1 tablespoon oil, if necessary. Serve patties with red pepper sauce.

Makes 6 servings

VARIATION Make 24 mini quinoa patties as an appetizer.

TOFU CAULIFLOWER FRIED RICE

- 3 tablespoons soy sauce
- 1 tablespoon plus 1 teaspoon minced fresh ginger, divided
- 2 teaspoons dark sesame oil
- 1 teaspoon packed brown sugar
- 1 teaspoon rice vinegar
- 1 package (14 ounces) firm tofu, drained and cut into 1-inch cubes
- 2 tablespoons vegetable oil, divided
- 1 yellow or sweet onion, chopped
- 1 carrot, chopped
- ½ cup frozen peas
- 2 cloves garlic, minced
- 1 package (12 ounces) frozen cauliflower rice
- 1 green onion, thinly sliced

1. Whisk soy sauce, 1 tablespoon ginger, sesame oil, brown sugar and vinegar in small bowl until well blended. Place tofu in quart-size resealable food storage bag. Pour marinade over tofu; seal bag, pressing out as much air as possible. Turn to coat tofu with marinade. Refrigerate 3 hours or overnight.
2. Drain tofu, reserving marinade. Heat 1 tablespoon vegetable oil in large cast iron skillet over high heat. Add tofu; cook and stir 3 to 5 minutes or until edges are browned. Transfer to bowl.
3. Heat remaining 1 tablespoon vegetable oil in same skillet. Add yellow onion and carrot; cook and stir 3 minutes or until softened. Add peas, garlic and remaining 1 teaspoon ginger; cook and stir 2 minutes or until peas are hot. Add frozen cauliflower rice and ¼ cup reserved marinade; cook and stir 5 minutes or until heated through.
4. Return tofu to skillet; cook and stir until heated through. Top with green onion.

Makes 4 servings

JAP CHAE (KOREAN GLASS NOODLE STIR-FRY)

- 5 ounces cellophane noodles (bean threads)
- ¼ cup soy sauce
- 1½ tablespoons dark sesame oil
- 3 cloves garlic, minced
- 2 teaspoons sugar
- 2 tablespoons vegetable oil
- 1 sweet potato (about 12 ounces), peeled and cut into thin strips
- 1 large carrot, cut into thin strips
- 1 small red bell pepper, cut into thin strips
- 1 small red onion, halved and thinly sliced
- 1 cup fresh shiitake mushrooms, stemmed and sliced
- 3 green onions, sliced
- 1 tablespoon sesame seeds, toasted

1. Soak noodles in hot water according to package directions. Whisk soy sauce, sesame oil, garlic and sugar in small bowl until well blended.
2. Heat vegetable oil in large cast iron skillet over high heat. Add sweet potato; cook and stir 3 minutes. Add carrot, bell pepper, onion and mushrooms; cook and stir 5 minutes or until vegetables are tender.
3. Drain noodles; add to skillet with soy sauce mixture. Cook 2 minutes or until sauce is absorbed. Stir in green onions and sesame seeds. Serve warm, cold or at room temperature.

Makes 6 servings

NOTE This classic Korean dish is typically made with sweet potato noodles (dangmyeon). In this recipe, chewy cellophane noodles are used instead. Leftover noodles make great lunches; they're good served cold, and their flavor gets even better with more time to blend.

FRIED GREEN TOMATO PARMESAN

- 2 cans (15 ounces each) tomato sauce
- 4 green tomatoes, thickly sliced into 3 slices each
- ½ teaspoon salt, divided
- Black pepper
- ½ cup all-purpose flour
- 1 teaspoon Italian seasoning
- 2 eggs
- 2 tablespoons water
- 1½ cups panko bread crumbs
- 4 tablespoons olive oil
- ½ cup shredded Parmesan cheese
- Shredded fresh basil
- Hot cooked spaghetti

1. Preheat oven to 350°F. Spread 1 cup tomato sauce in 9-inch square baking dish. Sprinkle one side of tomatoes with ¼ teaspoon salt; season lightly with pepper.
2. Combine flour, Italian seasoning and remaining ¼ teaspoon salt in shallow bowl. Whisk eggs and water in another shallow bowl. Place panko in third shallow bowl. Coat tomatoes with flour mixture. Dip in egg mixture, then in panko, pressing onto all sides to coat completely.
3. Heat 2 tablespoons oil in large cast iron skillet over medium-high heat. Add half of tomatoes; cook 3 minutes per side or until panko is golden brown. Arrange tomatoes in single layer in sauce in baking dish. Sprinkle 1 teaspoon cheese on each tomato; spread some sauce over tomatoes. Heat remaining 2 tablespoons oil in same skillet; cook remaining tomatoes 3 minutes per side until panko is golden brown. Stagger tomatoes in second layer over tomatoes in baking dish. Top each tomato with 1 teaspoon cheese; spread 1 cup sauce over top. Sprinkle with remaining cheese.
4. Bake 20 minutes or until cheese is melted and sauce is heated through. Heat remaining tomato sauce. Serve tomatoes with basil, spaghetti and sauce.

Makes 4 servings

TOFU IN PURGATORY

- 2 tablespoons olive oil
- 1 large onion, chopped
- 2 cloves garlic, minced
- 2 tablespoons tomato paste
- 1 teaspoon salt
- 1 teaspoon ground cumin
- 1 teaspoon ground coriander
- ½ teaspoon smoked paprika
- 1 can (28 ounces) diced tomatoes
- Crispy Toast (recipe follows)
- 1 package (about 12 ounces) firm silken tofu, cut into 8 cubes
- Shredded fresh basil

1. Heat oil in large cast iron skillet over medium-high heat. Add onion; cook and stir 5 minutes or until softened. Add garlic, tomato paste, salt, cumin, coriander and paprika; cook and stir 1 minute.
2. Stir in tomatoes; bring to a simmer. Reduce heat to medium-low; cook 20 minutes, stirring occasionally. Meanwhile, prepare Crispy Toast.
3. Make eight divots in sauce; add tofu cubes. Cover and cook 10 minutes to heat tofu. Sprinkle with basil; serve with toast.

Makes 4 servings

CRISPY TOAST Preheat oven to 400°F. Place 4 to 8 slices of French, Italian or sourdough bread on baking sheet. Brush olive oil over both sides of bread. Bake 8 to 10 minutes or until golden brown and crisp, turning once. Cut 2 garlic cloves in half; rub cut sides over one side of each toast.

CURRIED QUINOA BURGERS

- **½ cup quinoa, rinsed well in fine-mesh strainer**
- **½ cup red lentils, rinsed well in fine-mesh strainer**
- **1½ cups water**
- **3 tablespoons olive oil, divided**
- **1 medium onion, diced**
- **1 teaspoon coarse salt**
- **½ cup frozen peas**
- **3 cloves garlic, minced**
- **2 teaspoons curry powder**
- **1 egg**
- **6 hamburger buns**
- **Optional toppings: lettuce, sliced tomatoes, thinly sliced red onion, mango chutney**

1. Combine quinoa, lentils and water in large saucepan over medium-high heat; bring to a boil. Reduce heat to low; cover and cook 15 minutes or until quinoa is cooked and lentils are tender. Transfer to large bowl.
2. Heat 1 tablespoon oil in large cast iron skillet over medium-high heat. Add onion and salt; cook 6 minutes or until onion begins to soften. Add peas; cook over medium heat 4 minutes. Add garlic and curry powder; cook 30 seconds, stirring frequently. Add to quinoa mixture with egg; stir until blended. Cool mixture 15 minutes. Wipe out skillet.
3. Shape ½ cupfuls of quinoa mixture into individual patties about ½ inch wide and ½ inch thick.
4. Heat 1 tablespoon oil in same skillet over medium-high heat. Reduce heat to medium. Gently place patties in skillet; cook 4 to 5 minutes or until bottoms are well browned. Add remaining 1 tablespoon oil to skillet; turn patties and cook 4 to 5 minutes or until browned.
5. Serve burgers on buns with desired toppings.

Makes 6 servings

PEANUT BUTTER TOFU BOWL

SAUCE

- ¼ cup peanut butter
- ¼ cup hoisin sauce
- 1 tablespoon packed brown sugar
- 1 tablespoon dark sesame oil
- 1 tablespoon water
- 1½ teaspoons minced fresh ginger
- 1½ teaspoons unseasoned rice vinegar
- 1½ teaspoons soy sauce
- 1 clove garlic, minced
- ½ teaspoon sriracha sauce

BOWL

- 1 package (14 to 16 ounces) firm tofu, pressed, cut into 24 (1-inch) cubes
- ¼ cup cornstarch
- 2 tablespoons plus 1 teaspoon vegetable oil, divided
- 1 head bok choy
- 1 clove garlic, minced
- 1 tablespoon soy sauce
- 1 tablespoon rice vinegar
- 2 cups hot cooked rice
- Minced fresh cilantro and/or chopped peanuts (optional)

1. For sauce, combine peanut butter, hoisin sauce, brown sugar, sesame oil, 1 tablespoon water, ginger, 1½ teaspoons vinegar, 1½ teaspoons soy sauce, 1 clove garlic and sriracha in small saucepan; cook over medium-low heat 5 minutes, whisking frequently.
2. Combine tofu and cornstarch in large bowl; toss to coat. Heat 2 tablespoons vegetable oil in large cast iron skillet over high heat. Add tofu; cook without stirring 5 minutes or until well browned and crusted on bottom. Turn and cook 5 minutes or until browned. Cook 2 minutes, turning frequently until all sides of tofu are lightly browned. Add sauce; cook 1 minute or until tofu is glazed.
3. Meanwhile, separate leaves and stems of bok choy. Coarsely chop stems and leaves separately.
4. Heat remaining 1 teaspoon vegetable oil in medium skillet over medium-high heat. Add bok choy stems; cook and stir 3 minutes. Add bok choy leaves and 1 clove garlic; cook and stir 1 minute. Add 1 tablespoon soy sauce and 1 tablespoon vinegar; cook and stir 30 seconds.
5. Divide rice, tofu and bok choy among four bowls. Garnish with cilantro and peanuts.

Makes 4 servings

VEGETABLES & SIDES

BALSAMIC BUTTERNUT SQUASH

- **3 tablespoons olive oil**
- **2 tablespoons thinly sliced fresh sage (about 6 large leaves), divided**
- **1 medium butternut squash, peeled and cut into 1-inch pieces (4 to 5 cups)**
- **½ small red onion, cut in half and cut into ¼-inch slices**
- **1 teaspoon salt, divided**
- **2½ tablespoons balsamic vinegar**
- **¼ teaspoon black pepper**

1. Heat oil in large cast iron skillet over medium-high heat. Add 1 tablespoon sage; cook and stir 3 minutes.
2. Add squash, onion and ½ teaspoon salt; cook 6 minutes, stirring occasionally. Reduce heat to medium; cook 15 minutes without stirring.
3. Stir in vinegar, remaining ½ teaspoon salt and pepper; cook 10 minutes or until squash is tender, stirring occasionally. Stir in remaining 1 tablespoon sage; cook 1 minute.

Makes 4 servings

SPANIKOPITA PULL-APARTS

- **4 tablespoons (½ stick) butter, melted, divided**
- **12 frozen white dinner rolls (⅓ of 3-pound package),* thawed according to package directions**
- **1 package (10 ounces) frozen chopped spinach, thawed and squeezed dry**
- **4 green onions, finely chopped (about ¼ cup packed)**
- **1 clove garlic, minced**
- **1 teaspoon dried dill weed**
- **½ teaspoon salt**
- **⅛ teaspoon black pepper**
- **1 cup (4 ounces) crumbled feta cheese**
- **¾ cup (3 ounces) grated Monterey Jack cheese, divided**

If frozen dinner rolls are not available, substitute one 16-ounce loaf of frozen bread dough or pizza dough. Thaw according to package directions and divide into 12 pieces.

1. Brush large (10-inch) cast iron skillet with ½ tablespoon butter. Cut rolls in half to make 24 balls of dough.
2. Combine spinach, green onions, garlic, dill weed, salt and pepper in medium bowl; mix well to break apart spinach. Add feta, ½ cup Monterey Jack and remaining 3½ tablespoons butter; mix well.
3. Coat each ball of dough with spinach mixture; arrange in single layer in prepared skillet. Sprinkle any remaining spinach mixture between and over balls of dough. Cover and let rise in warm place about 40 minutes or until almost doubled in size.
4. Preheat oven to 350°F. Sprinkle remaining ¼ cup Monterey Jack over dough.
5. Bake 35 to 40 minutes or until golden brown. Serve warm.

Makes 24 rolls

SKILLET ROASTED ROOT VEGETABLES

- 1 sweet potato, peeled, cut in half lengthwise and cut crosswise into ½-inch slices
- 1 large red onion, cut into 1-inch wedges
- 2 parsnips, cut diagonally into 1-inch slices
- 2 carrots, cut diagonally into 1-inch slices
- 1 turnip, peeled, cut in half and cut into ½-inch slices
- 2½ tablespoons olive oil
- 1½ tablespoons honey
- 1½ tablespoons balsamic vinegar
- 1 teaspoon coarse salt
- 1 teaspoon dried thyme
- ¼ teaspoon ground red pepper
- ¼ teaspoon black pepper

1. Preheat oven to 400°F.
2. Combine all ingredients in large bowl; toss to coat.
3. Spread vegetables in single layer in large cast iron skillet.
4. Roast 1 hour or until vegetables are tender, stirring once halfway through cooking time.

Makes 4 servings

HUSH PUPPIES >>

- 1½ cups yellow cornmeal
- ½ cup all-purpose flour
- 2 teaspoons baking powder
- ¾ teaspoon salt
- 1 cup milk
- 1 small onion, minced
- 1 egg, lightly beaten
- Vegetable oil
- Ketchup (optional)

1. Combine cornmeal, flour, baking powder and salt in medium bowl; mix well. Add milk, onion and egg; whisk until well blended. Let batter stand 5 to 10 minutes.
2. Heat 1 inch of oil in large cast iron skillet over medium heat to 375°F; adjust heat to maintain temperature.
3. Drop batter by tablespoonfuls into hot oil. Cook, in batches, 2 minutes or until golden brown. Drain on paper towel-lined plate. Serve hush puppies warm with ketchup, if desired.

Makes about 24 hush puppies

CINNAMON APPLES

- ¼ cup (½ stick) butter
- 3 tart red apples such as Gala, Fuji or Honeycrisp (about 1½ pounds total), peeled and cut into ½-inch wedges
- ¼ cup packed brown sugar
- 1 teaspoon ground cinnamon
- ⅛ teaspoon ground nutmeg
- ⅛ teaspoon salt
- 1 tablespoon cornstarch

1. Melt butter in large cast iron skillet over medium-high heat. Add apples; cook 8 minutes or until tender, stirring occasionally.
2. Add brown sugar, cinnamon, nutmeg and salt; cook and stir 1 minute or until apples are glazed. Reduce heat to medium-low; stir in cornstarch until well blended.
3. Remove from heat; let stand 5 minutes for glaze to thicken. Stir again; serve immediately.

Makes 4 servings

SKILLET MAC AND CHEESE

- 1 pound uncooked cavatappi or rotini pasta
- 8 ounces thick-cut bacon, cut into ½-inch pieces
- ¼ cup finely chopped onion
- ¼ cup all-purpose flour
- 3½ cups whole milk
- 1 cup (4 ounces) shredded white Cheddar cheese
- 1 cup (4 ounces) shredded fontina cheese
- 1 cup (4 ounces) shredded Gruyère cheese
- ¾ cup grated Parmesan cheese, divided
- ½ teaspoon salt
- ½ teaspoon dry mustard
- ¼ teaspoon ground red pepper
- ¼ teaspoon black pepper
- ¼ cup panko bread crumbs

1. Preheat oven to 400°F. Cook pasta according to package directions until al dente; drain.
2. Meanwhile, cook bacon in large cast iron skillet until crisp; drain on paper towel-lined plate. Pour drippings into glass measuring cup, leaving thin coating on surface of skillet.
3. Heat 4 tablespoons drippings in large saucepan over medium-high heat. Add onion; cook and stir 4 minutes or until translucent. Add flour; cook and stir 5 minutes. Slowly add milk over medium-low heat, stirring constantly. Stir in Cheddar, fontina, Gruyère, ½ cup Parmesan, salt, mustard, red pepper and black pepper until smooth and well blended.
4. Add cooked pasta to saucepan; stir gently until coated with cheese sauce. Stir in bacon. Spread mixture in cast iron skillet.
5. Combine panko and remaining ¼ cup Parmesan in small bowl; sprinkle over pasta. Bake 30 minutes or until top is golden brown.

Makes 6 servings

SPIRALIZED POTATO LATKES

- 2 small *or* 1 large sweet potato (about 1 pound), peeled
- 1 russet potato (about 12 ounces), peeled
- 1 shallot, minced
- 3 eggs
- ⅓ cup all-purpose flour
- ½ teaspoon salt
- ¼ teaspoon baking powder
- ⅛ teaspoon ground nutmeg
- 1 cup vegetable oil for frying
- Applesauce and/or sour cream for serving

1. Cut potatoes in half; spiral with thin ribbon blade of spiralizer.
2. Pile potato strips loosely on cutting board; cut three times as if cutting into six wedges. Combine potatoes and shallot in large bowl.
3. Whisk eggs, flour, salt, baking powder and nutmeg in small bowl until well blended. Add to potatoes; mix well.
4. Heat oil in large cast iron skillet over medium-high heat until drop of batter sizzles. Working in batches, drop mixture by scant ½ cupfuls into hot oil; flatten slightly with bottom of measuring cup. Cook 3 minutes per side or until golden brown. Drain on paper towel-lined plate. Serve immediately with applesauce.

Makes 10 latkes

CAJUN RICE

- 2 cups uncooked long grain rice
- 4 cups water, divided
- 1¼ teaspoons salt, divided
- 4 green onions, finely chopped, green and white parts separated
- 12 ounces ground beef
- ½ cup finely chopped green bell pepper
- 1 teaspoon Cajun or Creole seasoning
- ½ teaspoon garlic powder
- ¼ teaspoon celery seed
- ¼ teaspoon ground red pepper
- ¼ teaspoon black pepper

1. Rinse rice in strainer under cold water; drain. Combine rice, 3¾ cups water and 1 teaspoon salt in medium saucepan; bring to a boil over medium-high heat. Reduce heat to low; cover and cook about 17 minutes or until liquid is absorbed and rice is tender but still firm. Remove from heat; let stand, covered, 5 minutes. Fluff rice with fork; stir in green parts of green onions.
2. Meanwhile, cook beef in large cast iron skillet over medium-high heat 5 minutes or until cooked through, stirring frequently. Remove to medium bowl; drain fat from skillet.
3. Add bell pepper, white parts of green onions, Cajun seasoning, garlic powder, celery seed, red pepper, black pepper and remaining ¼ teaspoon salt to skillet; cook and stir 2 minutes. Return beef to skillet; mix well.
4. Stir in rice and remaining ¼ cup water; cook over medium-low heat 15 minutes, stirring occasionally.

Makes 8 servings

POTATO AND CORNED BEEF CAKES

- **2 pounds russet potatoes, divided**
- **2 teaspoons salt, divided**
- **6 tablespoons all-purpose flour**
- **¼ cup whole milk**
- **1 egg, beaten**
- **½ teaspoon black pepper**
- **1 cup chopped corned beef (leftover or deli corned beef, about ⅓ pound), cut into ¼-inch pieces**
- **1 tablespoon butter**
- **1 tablespoon olive oil**
- **Chopped fresh parsley (optional)**

1. Peel half of potatoes; cut into 1-inch pieces. Place in medium saucepan; add 1 teaspoon salt and water to cover by 2 inches. Bring to a simmer over medium heat; cook 15 minutes or until tender.
2. Drain and rice potatoes into medium bowl.
3. Peel remaining half of potatoes; grate with box grater. Squeeze out and discard liquid from grated potatoes.
4. Add grated potatoes to riced potatoes in bowl; stir in flour, milk, egg, remaining 1 teaspoon salt and pepper. Stir in corned beef until well blended.
5. Heat butter and oil in large cast iron skillet over medium heat. Shape ⅓ cupfuls of potato mixture into patties; cook in batches 3 to 4 minutes per side or until golden brown. (Do not crowd patties in skillet.) Sprinkle with parsley, if desired.

Makes 10 cakes

RED CABBAGE WITH BACON AND MUSHROOMS

- 5 slices thick-cut bacon, chopped (about 8 ounces)
- 1 onion, chopped
- 1 package (8 ounces) cremini mushrooms, chopped (½-inch pieces)
- ¾ teaspoon dried thyme
- ½ medium red cabbage, cut into wedges, cored and cut crosswise into ¼-inch slices (about 7 cups)
- ¼ teaspoon salt
- ¼ teaspoon black pepper
- ⅔ cup chicken broth
- 3 tablespoons cider vinegar
- ¼ cup chopped walnuts, toasted*
- 3 tablespoons chopped fresh parsley

**To toast walnuts, cook in small skillet over medium heat 4 to 5 minutes or until lightly browned, stirring frequently.*

1. Cook bacon in large cast iron skillet over medium-high heat until crisp. Remove to paper towel-lined plate. Drain all but 1 tablespoon drippings from skillet.
2. Add onion to skillet; cook and stir 5 minutes or until softened. Add mushrooms and thyme; cook 6 minutes or until mushrooms begin to brown, stirring occasionally. Add cabbage, ¼ teaspoon salt and ¼ teaspoon pepper; cook 7 minutes or until cabbage is wilted.
3. Stir in broth, vinegar and half of bacon; bring to a boil. Reduce heat to low; cook, uncovered, 15 to 20 minutes or until cabbage is tender.
4. Stir in walnuts and parsley; season with additional salt and pepper, if necessary. Sprinkle with remaining bacon.

Makes 6 servings

HAGGERTY

- **8 slices bacon (about 8 ounces)**
- **3 onions, thinly sliced**
- **1½ cups (6 ounces) shredded Cheddar cheese, divided**
- **2 tablespoons butter, divided**
- **5 medium unpeeled red potatoes (about 1¼ pounds), very thinly sliced**
- **Salt and black pepper**

1. Preheat oven to 375°F.
2. Cook bacon in large cast iron skillet until crisp. Drain on paper towel-lined plate; crumble into medium bowl. Drain all but 1 tablespoon drippings from skillet.
3. Add onions to skillet; cook and stir over medium heat about 8 minutes or until translucent but not browned. Remove to bowl with bacon; mix well.
4. Reserve ¼ cup cheese; set aside. Melt 1 tablespoon butter in same skillet. Arrange one quarter of potato slices to cover bottom of skillet. Season with salt and pepper. Top with one third of bacon-onion mixture; sprinkle with one third of remaining cheese. Repeat layers twice. Top with remaining one quarter of potato slices; dot with remaining 1 tablespoon butter.
5. Cover with foil and bake 50 minutes. Uncover; bake 10 minutes or until potatoes are tender. *Turn oven to broil.* Broil 2 to 3 minutes or until lightly browned. Sprinkle with reserved ¼ cup cheese. Serve warm.

Makes 6 to 8 servings

TIP **Use a mandolin to slice the potatoes very thin (about ⅛ inch). Thicker pieces may require a longer cooking time.**

FLOUR TORTILLAS

2 cups all-purpose flour
¾ teaspoon salt
¾ teaspoon baking powder
⅔ cup warm water (105° to 115°F)
¼ cup vegetable oil

1. Combine flour, salt and baking powder in large bowl of stand mixer; mix with dough hook at low speed to combine. With mixer running at medium speed, add water and oil in thin, steady stream. Mix 2 minutes or until dough is well blended and smooth.
2. Turn out dough onto lightly floured surface; divide into 12 pieces. Shape dough into balls. Cover with clean kitchen towel; let rest at least 15 minutes.
3. Heat medium cast iron skillet over medium-high heat. Roll each piece of dough into very thin 6-inch circle on lightly floured surface with lightly floured rolling pin.
4. Working with one tortilla at at time, add to hot skillet; cook 1 minute. (Bottom should be golden brown in spots and top should be bubbly.) Turn and cook about 30 seconds or until tortilla is firm and beginning to brown in spots. Stack cooked tortillas; wrap in clean kitchen towel to keep soft and warm.

Makes 12 tortillas

TIP **Tortillas can be stored in a resealable food storage bag or an airtight container at room temperature overnight or refrigerated up to 1 week.**

MEXICAN CAULIFLOWER AND BEAN SKILLET

- 1 tablespoon olive oil
- 3 cups coarsely chopped cauliflower
- ¾ teaspoon salt
- ½ medium yellow onion, chopped
- 1 green bell pepper, chopped
- 1 clove garlic, minced
- 1 teaspoon chili powder
- ¾ teaspoon ground cumin
- Pinch ground red pepper
- 1 can (about 15 ounces) black beans, rinsed and drained
- 1 cup (4 ounces) shredded Cheddar-Jack cheese
- Salsa and sour cream

1. Heat oil in large cast iron skillet over medium-high heat. Add cauliflower and salt; cook and stir 5 minutes. Add onion, bell pepper, garlic, chili powder, cumin and red pepper; cook and stir 5 minutes or until cauliflower is tender.
2. Stir in beans; cook until beans are heated through. Remove from heat.
3. Sprinkle with cheese; fold in gently and let stand until cheese is melted. Serve with salsa and sour cream.

Makes 4 to 6 servings

SERVING SUGGESTION Serve over brown rice or with warm corn tortillas.

CRISPY SKILLET POTATOES >>

- 2 tablespoons olive oil
- 4 unpeeled red potatoes, cut into thin wedges
- ½ cup chopped onion
- 2 tablespoons lemon-pepper seasoning
- ½ teaspoon coarse salt
- Chopped fresh parsley (optional)

1. Heat oil in large cast iron skillet over medium heat. Add potatoes, onion, lemon-pepper seasoning and salt; cover and cook 25 to 30 minutes or until potatoes are tender and browned, turning occasionally.
2. Sprinkle with parsley, if desired, just before serving.

Makes 4 servings

SAUSAGE AND CHEDDAR CORN BREAD

- 1 tablespoon vegetable oil
- ½ pound bulk pork sausage
- 1 medium onion, diced
- 1 jalapeño pepper, diced
- 1 package (about 8 ounces) corn muffin mix
- 1 cup (4 ounces) shredded Cheddar cheese, divided
- ⅓ cup milk
- 1 egg

1. Heat oil in large cast iron skillet over medium heat. Brown sausage 6 to 8 minutes, stirring to break up meat. Add onion and jalapeño; cook and stir 5 minutes or until vegetables are softened. Remove sausage mixture to medium bowl.
2. Preheat oven to 350°F. Combine corn muffin mix, ½ cup cheese, milk and egg in separate medium bowl. Pour batter into skillet; top with sausage mixture. Sprinkle with remaining ½ cup cheese.
3. Bake 20 to 25 minutes or until edges are lightly browned. Cut into wedges.

Makes 10 servings

DESSERTS

CINNAMON ROLL-TOPPED SKILLET COBBLER

- 1 tablespoon cornstarch
- 2 tablespoons lemon juice
- 5 apples (about 2 pounds), peeled and cut into ½-inch pieces
- ½ cup packed brown sugar
- ¾ teaspoon ground cinnamon
- ⅛ teaspoon ground ginger
- 3 tablespoons butter
- ½ cup coarsely chopped pecans
- 1 cup fresh blueberries
- 1 package (13 ounces) refrigerated flaky cinnamon rolls with icing

1. Preheat oven to 350°F.
2. Stir cornstarch into lemon juice in small bowl until smooth. Combine apples, brown sugar, cinnamon and ginger in large bowl; mix well. Add cornstarch mixture; stir to coat.
3. Melt butter in large (12-inch) cast iron skillet over medium heat. Add apple mixture and pecans; press into layer that covers bottom of skillet. Sprinkle with blueberries.
4. Bake 20 minutes. Remove skillet from oven. Separate cinnamon rolls; reserve icing. Arrange cinnamon rolls over warm fruit mixture.
5. Bake 20 to 25 minutes or until filling is bubbly and cinnamon rolls are deep golden brown. Drizzle with icing. Let stand 5 minutes before serving.

Makes 8 servings

WARM MIXED BERRY PIE

- **2 packages (12 ounces each) frozen mixed berries**
- **⅓ cup sugar**
- **3 tablespoons cornstarch**
- **2 teaspoons grated orange peel**
- **¼ teaspoon ground ginger**
- **1 refrigerated pie crust (half of 14-ounce package)**

1. Preheat oven to 350°F.
2. Combine berries, sugar, cornstarch, orange peel and ginger in large bowl; toss gently to coat. spread evenly in large cast iron skillet.
3. Roll out crust into 12-inch circle on lightly floured surface. Place crust over fruit mixture; flute edge as desired. Cut several slits in crust to allow steam to escape.
4. Bake 1 hour or until crust is golden brown. Let pie stand 1 hour before serving.

Makes 8 servings

CHOCOLATE CHIP PIZZA COOKIE

- 2 cups all-purpose flour
- 1 teaspoon baking soda
- 1 teaspoon salt
- ¾ cup (1½ sticks) butter, softened
- 1 cup packed brown sugar
- ¼ cup granulated sugar
- 2 eggs
- 1 teaspoon vanilla
- 1 package (about 11 ounces) chocolate chips
- Vanilla ice cream

1. Preheat oven to 400°F. Spray three 6-inch cast iron skillets, cake pans or deep-dish pizza pans with nonstick cooking spray.*
2. Combine flour, baking soda and salt in medium bowl; mix well. Beat butter, brown sugar and granulated sugar in large bowl with electric mixer at medium speed about 3 minutes or until creamy. Beat in eggs and vanilla until well blended. Gradually beat in flour mixture at low speed just until blended.
3. Reserve ¼ cup chocolate chips for tops of cookies, if desired. Stir remaining chocolate chips into dough. Spread dough evenly in prepared skillets; sprinkle with reserved chocolate chips.
4. Bake about 15 minutes or until top and edges are deep golden brown but center is still slightly soft. Top with ice cream. Serve warm.

**If you don't have three skillets or pans, you can bake one cookie at a time. Refrigerate the dough between batches and make sure the skillet is completely cool before adding more dough. (Clean and spray the skillet again before adding each new batch.)*

Makes 3 pizza cookies (2 to 3 servings each)

GINGER PLUM TART

- 1 refrigerated pie crust (half of 14-ounce package)
- 1¾ pounds plums, cut into ½-inch slices
- ½ cup plus 1 teaspoon sugar, divided
- 1½ tablespoons all-purpose flour
- 1½ teaspoons ground ginger
- ¼ teaspoon ground cinnamon
- ⅛ teaspoon salt
- 1 egg
- 2 teaspoons water

1. Preheat oven to 400°F. Let pie crust stand at room temperature 10 minutes. Combine plums, ½ cup sugar, flour, ginger, cinnamon and salt in large bowl; toss to coat.
2. Roll out crust on lightly floured surface into 14-inch circle. Transfer crust to large (10-inch) cast iron skillet.
3. Mound plum mixture in center of crust, leaving 2-inch border around fruit. Fold crust up over filling, pleating as necessary and gently pressing crust into fruit to secure.
4. Beat egg and water in small bowl; brush over crust. Sprinkle with remaining 1 teaspoon sugar.*
5. Bake about 45 minutes or until crust is golden brown. Cool on wire rack. Serve warm or at room temperature.

**To add sparkle and extra crunch to the tart, use sparkling or coarse sugar to sprinkle on top instead of granulated sugar.*

Makes 6 to 8 servings

APPLE CRANBERRY CRUMBLE

- 4 large apples (about 1⅓ pounds), peeled and cut into ¼-inch slices
- 2 cups fresh or frozen cranberries
- ⅓ cup granulated sugar
- 6 tablespoons all-purpose flour, divided
- 1 teaspoon apple pie spice, divided
- ¼ teaspoon salt, divided
- ½ cup chopped walnuts
- ¼ cup old-fashioned oats
- 2 tablespoons packed brown sugar
- ¼ cup (½ stick) butter, cut into small pieces

1. Preheat oven to 375°F.
2. Combine apples, cranberries, granulated sugar, 2 tablespoons flour, ½ teaspoon apple pie spice and ⅛ teaspoon salt in large bowl; toss to coat. Spoon into medium (8- to 9-inch) cast iron skillet.
3. Combine remaining 4 tablespoons flour, ½ teaspoon apple pie spice, ⅛ teaspoon salt, walnuts, oats and brown sugar in medium bowl; mix well. Cut in butter with pastry blender or two knives until mixture resembles coarse crumbs. Sprinkle over fruit mixture in skillet.
4. Bake 50 to 60 minutes or until filling is bubbly and topping is lightly browned.

Makes 4 servings

INDEX

INDEX

INDEX

METRIC CONVERSION CHART

VOLUME MEASUREMENTS (dry)

$\frac{1}{8}$ teaspoon = 0.5 mL
$\frac{1}{4}$ teaspoon = 1 mL
$\frac{1}{2}$ teaspoon = 2 mL
$\frac{3}{4}$ teaspoon = 4 mL
1 teaspoon = 5 mL
1 tablespoon = 15 mL
2 tablespoons = 30 mL
$\frac{1}{4}$ cup = 60 mL
$\frac{1}{3}$ cup = 75 mL
$\frac{1}{2}$ cup = 125 mL
$\frac{2}{3}$ cup = 150 mL
$\frac{3}{4}$ cup = 175 mL
1 cup = 250 mL
2 cups = 1 pint = 500 mL
3 cups = 750 mL
4 cups = 1 quart = 1 L

VOLUME MEASUREMENTS (fluid)

1 fluid ounce (2 tablespoons) = 30 mL
4 fluid ounces ($\frac{1}{2}$ cup) = 125 mL
8 fluid ounces (1 cup) = 250 mL
12 fluid ounces (1$\frac{1}{2}$ cups) = 375 mL
16 fluid ounces (2 cups) = 500 mL

WEIGHTS (mass)

$\frac{1}{2}$ ounce = 15 g
1 ounce = 30 g
3 ounces = 90 g
4 ounces = 120 g
8 ounces = 225 g
10 ounces = 285 g
12 ounces = 360 g
16 ounces = 1 pound = 450 g

DIMENSIONS

$\frac{1}{16}$ inch = 2 mm
$\frac{1}{8}$ inch = 3 mm
$\frac{1}{4}$ inch = 6 mm
$\frac{1}{2}$ inch = 1.5 cm
$\frac{3}{4}$ inch = 2 cm
1 inch = 2.5 cm

OVEN TEMPERATURES

250°F = 120°C
275°F = 140°C
300°F = 150°C
325°F = 160°C
350°F = 180°C
375°F = 190°C
400°F = 200°C
425°F = 220°C
450°F = 230°C

BAKING PAN SIZES

Utensil	Size in Inches/Quarts	Metric Volume	Size in Centimeters
Baking or Cake Pan (square or rectangular)	8×8×2	2 L	20×20×5
	9×9×2	2.5 L	23×23×5
	12×8×2	3 L	30×20×5
	13×9×2	3.5 L	33×23×5
Loaf Pan	8×4×3	1.5 L	20×10×7
	9×5×3	2 L	23×13×7
Round Layer Cake Pan	8×1½	1.2 L	20×4
	9×1½	1.5 L	23×4
Pie Plate	8×1¼	750 mL	20×3
	9×1¼	1 L	23×3
Baking Dish or Casserole	1 quart	1 L	—
	1½ quart	1.5 L	—
	2 quart	2 L	—